THE HOW AND WHY WONDER BOOK OF
AIRPLANES AND THE STORY OF FLIGHT

(Originally published under the title
The How and Why Wonder Book of Flight)

Written by HAROLD JOSEPH HIGHLAND, B.S., M.S., Ph.D.
Associate Professor, College of Business Administration,
Long Island University

Illustrated by GEORGE J. ZAFFO

Editorial Production: DONALD D. WOLF

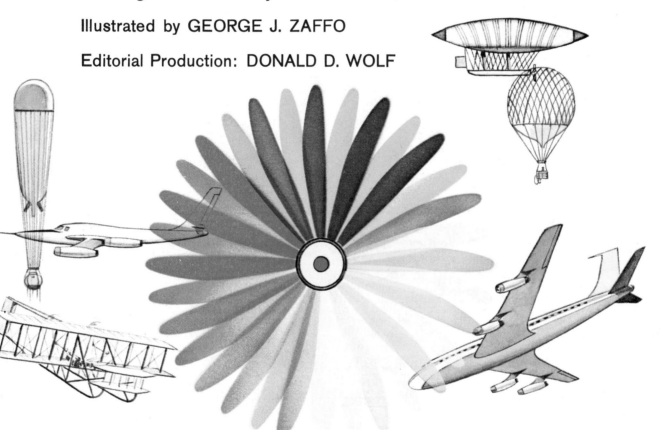

Edited under the supervision of
Dr. Paul E. Blackwood.
Washington, D. C.

Text and illustrations approved by
Oakes A. White, Brooklyn Children's Museum, Brooklyn, New York

J.G. Ferguson Publishing Company
Chicago

Introduction

Scientists are filled with curiosity and this leads them to search for answers through exploration and experiment. This *How and Why Wonder Book* amply demonstrates how, over the years, the search for ways to move through the air has led to present-day miracles of flight. The book will help young scientists to widen their horizons of discovery about the unending efforts to conquer and explore space.

To fly like a bird has always been a hope of man. We know this from legend, mythology and recorded history. The hope has burned in man's dreams and challenged him to make the attempt. First it seemed like a dream of improbable fulfillment. Then gradually, from fumbling beginnings, success was achieved. Man flew! And now, in many ways, he flies better than the birds—higher and faster and beyond the air.

The How and Why Wonder Book of Airplanes and the Story of Flight helps the reader to relive the fascinating story of man's increasing mastery of the air from early attempts to present-day accomplishments. It takes the reader from the first flights of balloons, which merely drifted with the wind, to the *Apollo* moon missions. Here are answers to many questions about early types of planes, jets, missiles and rockets. Why does an airplane fly? What is the jet stream? How do pilots navigate in bad weather? And many others.

Everyone who is excited about living in the Space Age, at a time when man continues his effort to explore the solar system, should have this book of basic information about flight for reading and reference.

Paul E. Blackwood

Dr. Blackwood is a professional employee in the U. S. Office of Education. This book was edited by him in his private capacity and no official support or endorsement by the Office of Education is intended or should be inferred.

Library of Congress Catalog Card No.: 73-124652
(Originally published under the title
The How and Why Wonder Book of Flight)

ISBN: 0-89434-076-X (set)

Science Library © 1987 J.G. Ferguson Publishing Company
Chicago

CONTENTS

Man gave the power of flight to gods and sacred animals. The winged bull is an Assyrian sculpture of the ninth century B.C.

The sphinx, a symbol of Egyptian royalty, was adopted by the Greeks. But it was given wings and served as tomb sculpture in the sixth century B.C.

This detail from a Greek vase of the fourth century B.C. shows the mythical hero Bellerophon mounted on his winged horse Pegasus. Together, they slew the dreaded Chimera. Sculptures similar to these are exhibited at the Metropolitan Museum of Art, New York.

Dreams of Flight

The story of man's dream of flight, of his desire to reach the stars, is as old as mankind itself. It is easy to imagine that prehistoric man, faced with a fierce, attacking monster, yearned to spring up and fly away just like a bird.

In ancient folklore and religions, we have ample proof of this desire to fly. But desires and dreams cannot lift a man off the earth, and so the wondrous ability to fly was reserved for his gods. Each of the gods had some means of flight. In ancient Greece, Phaeton, son of Helios, the sun god, drove the wild horses that pulled the sun chariot. Mercury, the messenger of the gods, had a winged helmet and winged sandals. The

Out of man's ancient dream of flight came this extension of his desire — a winged lion (Middle Ages).

The woodcut by the German painter and engraver, Albrecht Dürer, depicts Daedalus and Icarus fleeing the island of Crete. But Icarus perished in the sea.

winged horse, Pegasus, was able to fly faster, farther and higher than any bird.

The dream of flight was universal. In ancient Egypt and Babylonia, they pictured winged bulls, winged lions and even men with wings. The ancient Chinese, Greeks, Aztecs of Central America, Iroquois of North America, all shared this dream.

According to Greek legend, Daedalus,

Who was the first man to fly?

the Athenian inventor, was the first man to fly. He and his son, Icarus, had been imprisoned on the island of Crete by King Minos. In order to escape, Daedalus shaped wings of wax into which he stuck bird feathers.

During their flight, Icarus flew too high and the sun melted the wax. He was drowned in the sea, and that body of water is still called the Icarian Sea in honor of the first man to lose his life in flying. The father is supposed to have continued his flight and reached Sicily, several hundred miles away.

There is also an English legend of King Bladud who, during his reign in the ninth century B.C., used wings to fly. But his flight was short-lived and he fell to his death.

A Frenchman named Besnier claimed that he flew the above contraption in the late seventeenth century.

De Lana's air boat was held aloft by four spheres.

The dream of flying continued, but in all the legends, the flier rose like a bird only to fall like a stone. It was more than twenty-six hundred years after King Bladud's flight that men flew up into the air and returned to earth safely.

The first man to approach flying on a

What is ethereal air?

scientific basis was Roger Bacon, an Englishman who lived during the thirteenth century. He envisioned the air about us as a sea, and he believed that a balloon could float on the air just as a boat did on water. His balloon, or air boat, was to be filled with *ethereal air* so that it might float on the air sea. We do not know what Bacon meant by ethereal air; yet, many still credit him with the basic concept of balloon flight.

Almost four hundred years later, Francesco de Lana, an Italian priest, applied Bacon's principle of air flight. He designed a boat, complete with mast

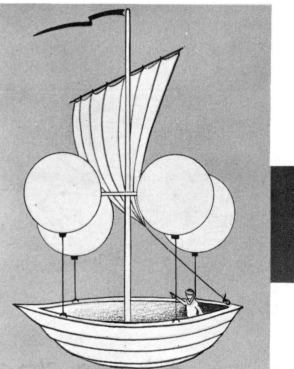

6

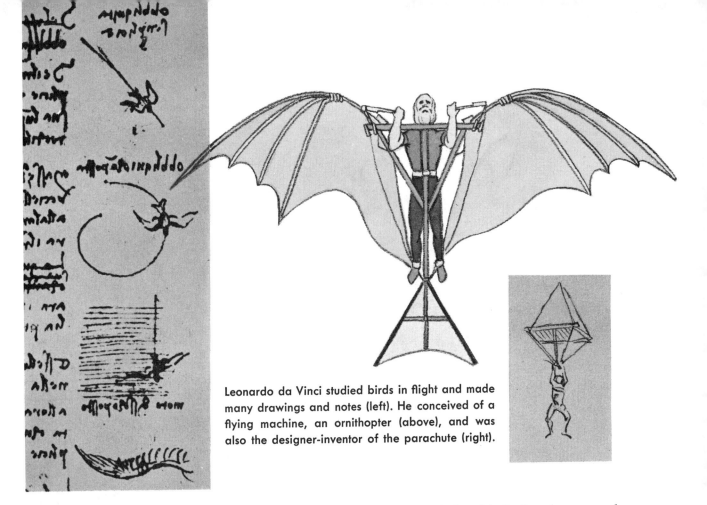

Leonardo da Vinci studied birds in flight and made many drawings and notes (left). He conceived of a flying machine, an ornithopter (above), and was also the designer-inventor of the parachute (right).

and sail, which would be held in the air by four hollow spheres. Each of the four balls was to be 20 feet in diameter and made of very thin copper. The air was to be removed from the balls so that they could float in the sky and lift the boat into the air.

De Lana's boat was never built since it was not possible to make spheres of such thin metal and such size in those days. Even if they had been built, the thin spheres would have been crushed by the pressure of the atmosphere.

Leonardo da Vinci was not only the

What is an ornithopter?

greatest mathematician of the fifteenth century, but also a noted painter, architect, sculptor, engineer and musician. After studying the flight of birds and the movement of the air,

he reasoned that birds flew because they flapped their wings and that it was possible for man to do the same. Da Vinci designed the *ornithopter* (or-ni-THOP-ter), a flapping-wing flying machine. The wings were to be moved by a man's arms and legs.

Ornithopters were tried by many men. Robert Hooke experimented with this means of flight in England about 1650. He claimed he succeeded in flying, but he also wrote of his great difficulties to remain in the air. He is the first man who recognized that feathers were not needed for flight.

Many men tried and failed to fly with the ornithopter. It was not until 1890 that Octave Chanute discovered why this method would never succeed — man could not develop sufficient power with only his arms and legs.

The first balloon flights were made in 1783 when the Montgolfier brothers used heated air to make an ornate balloon rise.

One of the memorable early balloon flights was made by J. A. C. Charles, a French physicist, and one of the Robert brothers. The flight lasted over two hours, reaching a two-mile height.

The Age of Aerostatics

In 1643, Evangelista Torricelli demonstrated that the earth's atmosphere is more than just empty space. With his barometer, he proved that the atmosphere has weight and density, just like any gas. This discovery was the beginning of the science of *aerostatics*. Aerostatics (aero-STAT-ics) is the study of how an object is supported in the air by buoy-

How did aerostatics help man to fly?

ancy; that is, its ability to float in air as a boat floats on water.

A milestone in this new science was reached ten years before the Declaration of Independence. Henry Cavendish, an English scientist, mixed iron, tin and zinc shavings with oil of vitriol and discovered a new gas which was lighter than air. Cavendish's "inflammable air" was later named "hydrogen" by the French chemist, Lavoisier.

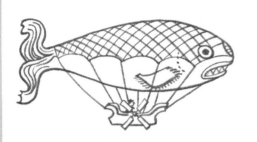

This fishlike flying contraption was constructed in France in the early 1800's, but it never flew.

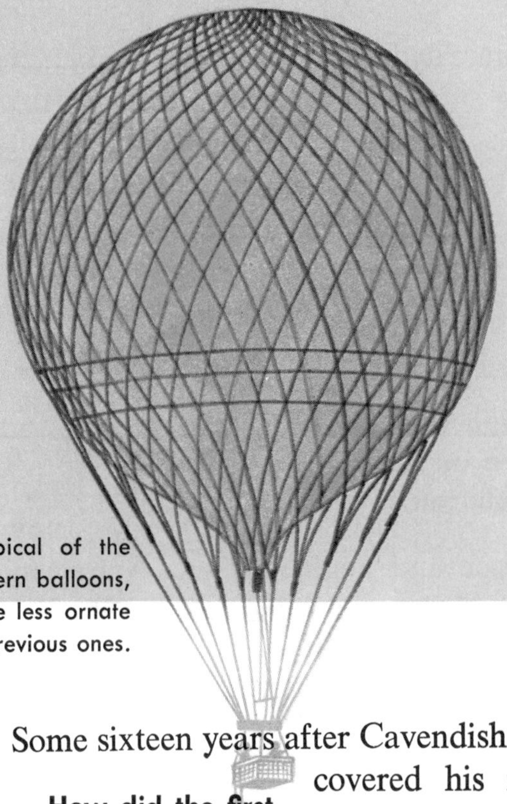

s is typical of the
ly modern balloons,
ch were less ornate
n the previous ones.

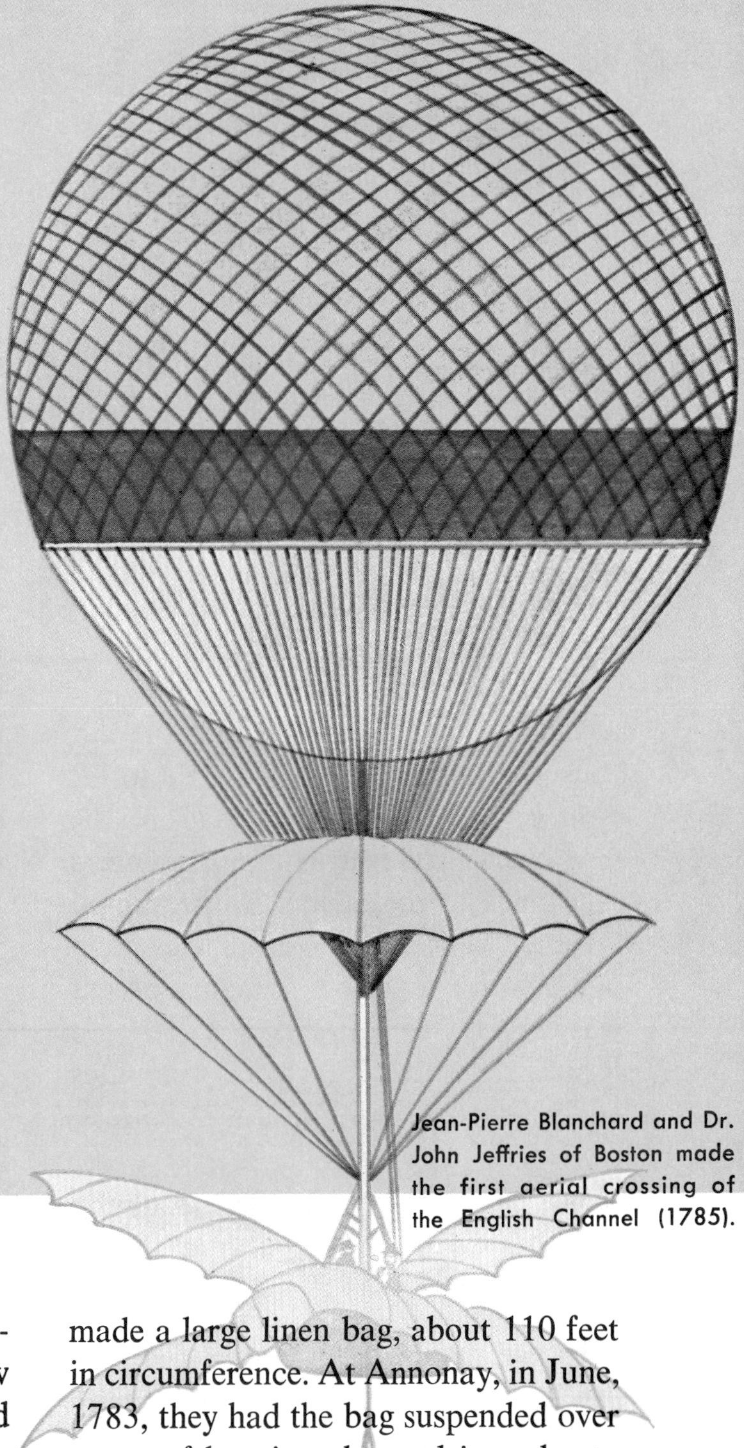

Jean-Pierre Blanchard and Dr. John Jeffries of Boston made the first aerial crossing of the English Channel (1785).

Some sixteen years after Cavendish discovered his new gas, Joseph and Jacques Montgolfier, French ornithoptists, were fascinated by watching smoke travel up from the fireplace through the chimney. They conceived the idea of making a smoke cloud which would fly in the air. They took a lightweight bag, filled it with smoke, and watched it float through the air.

How did the first balloonists fly?

After numerous experiments, they made a large linen bag, about 110 feet in circumference. At Annonay, in June, 1783, they had the bag suspended over a pan of burning charcoal in order to fill it with smoke. The smoke-filled bag rose almost 6,000 feet into the air and stayed aloft for ten minutes. It fell to earth a couple of miles away as the heated gas eventually cooled. A man-made object had actually flown.

With the French Royal Academy of Sciences, the brothers built a larger balloon, 41 feet in diameter. It carried

9

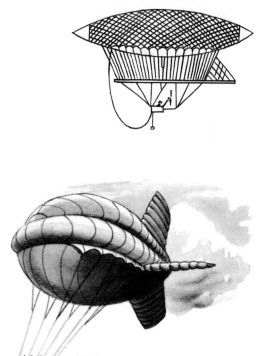

some 400 to 500 pounds into the air, thus proving that it was possible to lift a man. On September 19, 1783, the new balloon carried its first passengers — a duck, a rooster and a sheep, and returned them safely to earth. Less than one month later, the first human ascent was made. Jean Francois Pilâtre de Rozier stayed aloft for over 4 minutes and reached a height of almost 85 feet.

Shortly after Pilâtre de Rozier took the first balloon flight, J. A. C. Charles, a French physicist, filled a rubber-coated silk balloon with hydrogen, which Cavendish had discovered. This balloon rose more rapidly than the earlier ones, remained in flight for almost 45 minutes, and landed over 16 miles away. Professor Charles raced after the balloon, but when he arrived he found the peasants using pitchforks to kill the unknown "monster."

Why did the hydrogen balloon fly?

The *Charlière,* as hydrogen balloons were called for many years, rose rapidly because hydrogen is considerably lighter than smoke or air. The weight of the air in a balloon that is about 3½ feet in diameter is 8 pounds. The weight of hydrogen in a similar balloon is only ½ pound.

The greatest of the early balloonists was Francois Blanchard, who demonstrated balloon flying all over Europe and made the first American balloon flight on January 9, 1793. His most famous flight was across the English Channel in 1785, when he established the first international air mail on record.

Who were other famous early balloonists?

Another famous early balloonist was Captain Coutelle of the French Revolutionary Army, who manned the first

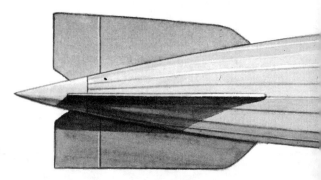

The zeppelin had a metal frame in which "bags" of hydrogen were used to make the craft "float."

balloon used in warfare. In 1794, at the battle of Fleurus, the captain signaled information to General Jourdan, who was able to take advantage of the shifting battle situation and emerged victorious.

The early balloons consisted of an inflated bag to which an open basket, or *gondola* (GON-do-la), was attached by ropes. To make the balloon go higher into the air, the "pilot" lightened its weight by dropping bags of sand, which were secured to the sides of the gondola. To make the balloon descend, he opened a valve and let some of the gas escape. The balloon rose into the air, but there was no way to control its flight. Once aloft, the balloon — and the men with it — were at the mercy of the winds.

How does a dirigible differ from a balloon?

The *dirigible* (DIR-i-gi-ble), or airship as it is sometimes called, can be steered. It consists of an elongated, gas-filled bag with cars, or gondolas, below for passengers and power. The dirigible takes advantage of the wind, but also uses motor-driven propellers. The early dirigibles used a sliding weight to make them go up or down. Pushing the weight toward the front pointed the nose of the airship down; conversely, with the weight toward the back, the nose pointed upward. Later dirigibles used horizontal tail fins to direct their upward and downward movement. Vertical tail fins were used to steer them right and left.

In 1852, almost seventy years after the first Montgolfier balloon rose over Annonay, a French engineer, Henri Giffard, built the first successful dirigible. Shaped like a cigar, it was 143 feet long and was powered by a 3-horsepower steam engine with a propeller attached to the gondola. Because of its low speed, about six miles per hour, this airship was pushed backward in a strong wind.

When did the first dirigible fly?

The first dirigible which could be accurately controlled and guided was *Airship Number One,* built by Alberto Santos-Dumont, a Brazilian millionaire living in France. In 1901, he flew his airship around the Eiffel Tower in Paris.

The early dirigibles were nonrigid; that is, they were long gas-filled bags. A gondola and powered propeller were attached. When longitudinal framing, running the length of the bag, was used as reinforcement, the semi-rigid dirigible was created.

What is a zeppelin?

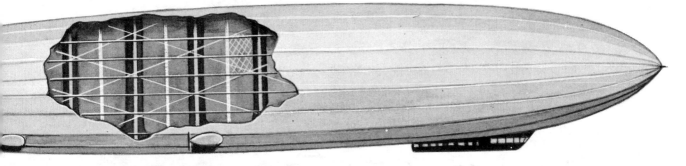

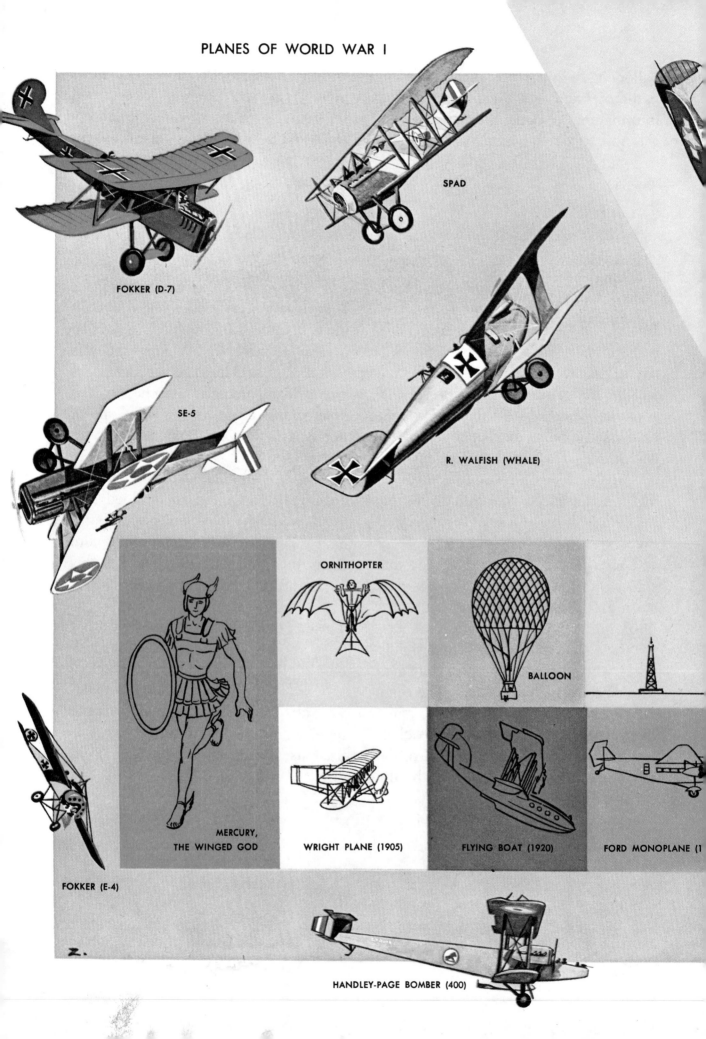

PLANES OF WORLD WAR I

FOKKER (D-7)

SPAD

SE-5

R. WALFISH (WHALE)

MERCURY, THE WINGED GOD

ORNITHOPTER

BALLOON

WRIGHT PLANE (1905)

FLYING BOAT (1920)

FORD MONOPLANE (1

FOKKER (E-4)

HANDLEY-PAGE BOMBER (400)

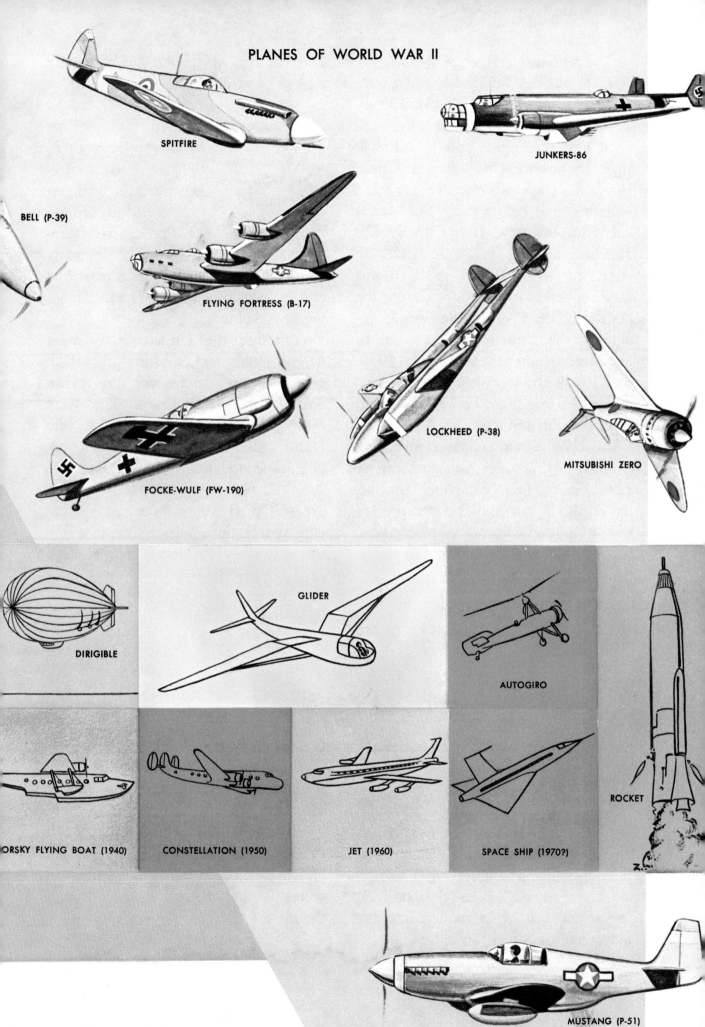

PLANES OF WORLD WAR II

SPITFIRE

JUNKERS-86

BELL (P-39)

FLYING FORTRESS (B-17)

LOCKHEED (P-38)

MITSUBISHI ZERO

FOCKE-WULF (FW-190)

DIRIGIBLE

GLIDER

AUTOGIRO

ROCKET

ORSKY FLYING BOAT (1940)

CONSTELLATION (1950)

JET (1960)

SPACE SHIP (1970?)

MUSTANG (P-51)

The rigid dirigible, or *zeppelin* (ZEP-pe-lin), was first built by Count Ferdinand von Zeppelin of Germany in 1899. This type, as contrasted with the nonrigid and semi-rigid, had a complete rigid framework covered with fabric. Inside the frame were several gas-filled balloons, and below the frame was a cabin for the crew. It was nearly 420 feet long and 38 feet in diameter.

During World War I, the Germans used zeppelins to drop bombs from the sky. After the war, other countries, including the United States, began to build zeppelin-type airships. In 1919, the British R-34 made the first transatlantic airship flight between England and the United States.

In 1929, the Graf Zeppelin took about ten days (flying time), traveling almost 22,000 miles, to go completely around the earth. Bigger and faster zeppelins were built, and they carried passengers, freight and mail to many sections of the world. The largest of these was the *Hindenburg,* which was 812 feet long and 135 feet in diameter.

Two factors contributed to the decline of the zeppelins. First, those filled with hydrogen were very dangerous, since hydrogen explodes and burns. The last hydrogen-filled zeppelin seen outside of Germany was the *Hindenburg,* which exploded and burned in May, 1937, while landing at Lakehurst, New Jersey.

Why did the zeppelin disappear?

Although the United States used *helium* (HE-li-um), a natural gas which does not burn, its airships, the *Akron* and *Macon,* were both lost. They were destroyed by bad weather, the second factor which caused the decline of zeppelin-type airships.

Small, nonrigid airships, or blimps, are still used for offshore anti-submarine patrol duty and to explore the edges of space, but large, rigid airships are part of history.

The Air Pioneers

Sir George Cayley has been called the father of *aeronautics* (aer-o-NAU-tics). This is the science of flight, including the principles and techniques of building and flying balloons, airships and airplanes, as well as *aerodynamics* (aer-o-dy-NAM-ics), the science of air in motion and the movement of bodies through the air.

Who is the father of aeronautics?

This early nineteenth century Englishman denounced ornithopters as impractical. Drawing upon an earlier discovery, Cayley decided that it would be possible to make a plane fly through the air if the plane were light enough, and if air could be forced against its wings by moving the plane through the air.

He solved the problem of making the

plane light by using diagonal bracing to reinforce the wings and body instead of using solid pieces of wood. The second problem, moving the ship through the air, was to be solved by a propeller-driven engine. Since there was no engine light enough or powerful enough, Cayley designed his own. It was an internal combustion engine which would use "oil of tar," or gasoline, as we now call it. But the fuel was too costly and Cayley was forced to abandon his engine. It was not until almost a hundred years later that such an engine was successfully built.

Sir George Cayley, father of aeronautics, built a successful glider in 1804, but he was unable to build a powered aircraft. His designs, however, were good.

Powered flight really started with William Henson and John Stringfellow.

When did the first powered airplane fly?

Using Cayley's principles, these two Englishmen designed an *aerial steam carriage* in 1842. Many of their ideas were practical, but they, too, were ahead of their time — there was no adequate engine.

In 1848, Stringfellow, working alone, built a model 10 feet long with a batlike wing. It had an engine which weighed less than 9 pounds and powered two propellers. It made short, sustained flights, flying as much as 40 yards. It was only a model, but it was real, powered flight.

The immediate ancestor of the successful powered airplane was the glider. It is a heavier-than-air machine *without* an engine. The glider uses air currents to sustain its flight. In calm weather, it can be launched

How does a glider fly?

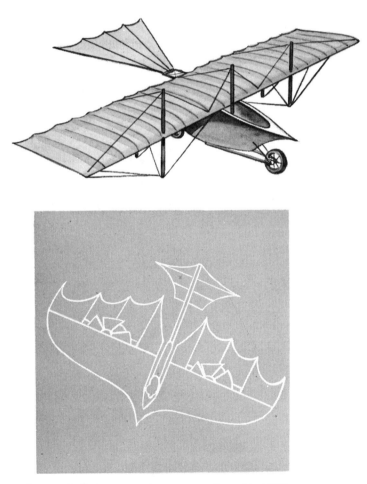

Powered flight came closer to reality with William Samuel Henson and John Stringfellow. They designed and flew the first powered models. But they were unable to build an engine to power a full-size plane.

from a high hilltop to obtain the needed forward thrust. The air rushing past its wings creates the necessary upward lift to counteract the gravitational force. The glider floats on the air and gradually descends to the ground.

In strong winds, the glider can be launched uphill so that it is picked up by the strong currents. It soars into the sky and continues to fly until the wind currents can no longer sustain it.

The greatest contribution in this field was made by Otto and Gustav Lilienthal. While still in high school in Germany, Otto built his first glider. It had wings that measured 6 by 3 feet each. In 1891, in Anklam, Germany, Otto made the first successful glider flight.

The brothers, noticing that birds took off *into* the wind, did the same with their gliders. They built many monoplane (single wing) and biplane (double wing) gliders and made over two thousand successful flights.

Perhaps Otto Lilienthal could have flown an airplane if a successful engine were available. In his attempt to develop such an engine, Otto lost his life. His experimental engine failed in flight and the airplane crashed.

Who made the first successful powered flight? Professor Langley, mathematician, physicist and Director of the Smithsonian Institution in Washington, D. C., was the last great air pioneer who failed to fly a plane. Using models, he supplied the answers to several problems which had to be solved before flying could be successful.

Early in the Spanish-American War, President McKinley asked Langley to develop a flying machine. Langley's assistant, Charles Manly, designed and built the first radial engine — the cylinders are built in a circle around the crankshaft. The engine used gasoline as fuel — it was Cayley's dream come true, almost a hundred years later.

Langley's *aerodrome* (AER-o-drome), as he called his plane, failed to fly on its second test on October 7, 1903. But some two months later, on December 17, 1903, at Kitty Hawk, North Carolina, the Wright brothers made the first successful flight.

Wilbur and Orville Wright were bicycle manufacturers from Dayton, Ohio, who built and flew gliders as early as 1900. After extensive work

The brothers Otto and Gustav Lilienthal paved the way for modern aviation. They built many gliders which flew successfully, and attempted powered flight. Otto was killed while testing a glider to which was attached a motor run by carbon dioxide.

on models, tested in wind tunnels, the Wright brothers designed and built their engine — a 4-cylinder model, weighing about 200 pounds, which developed 12 horsepower. They mounted this engine in a reinforced glider, and at Kitty Hawk, Orville Wright made four successful flights in one day. The first lasted only 12 seconds during which time the plane flew 120 feet. On the fourth flight the plane covered 852 feet and remained in the air for 59 seconds.

Despite its advanced engine, Samuel Langley's plane failed to fly. The gasoline engine, weighing less than three pounds per horsepower, was unequaled for twenty years.

How did early aviation progress?

The Wright brothers worked in Dayton for five years after their success at Kitty Hawk. In 1908, they developed a military airplane for the U. S. Army and in 1909, they demonstrated that a plane was capable of carrying a passenger. It flew at 40 miles per hour, carrying enough gasoline for a flight of 125 miles.

All over Europe and America, successful airplanes were demonstrated. In 1909, Louis Blériot flew across the English Channel. In that same year, the first international air meet was held at Rheims, France with thirty-eight airplanes participating. At that meet, Glenn H. Curtiss, an airplane designer and builder from the United States, established a speed record of 47.8 miles per hour. Hubert Latham set an altitude record of 508 feet, while Henri Farman, a Frenchman, established the endurance record of 3 hours and 5 minutes. The

On December 17, 1903, at Kitty Hawk, North Carolina, the first heavier-than-air plane was flown by the Wrights.

Louis Blériot set a new record when, in 1909, he flew across the English Channel in this small plane.

The first plane to take off and land on a ship at sea was flown by Eugene Ely, an American (1910).

longest flight at the meet was 118 miles.

One year later, in 1910, Eugene Ely, an American pilot, demonstrated a flight which eventually led to aircraft carriers. His plane took off from the cruiser *U.S.S. Birmingham* and landed on the battleship *U.S.S. Pennsylvania*.

The outbreak of World War I spurred the development of the airplane. Although attention was concentrated on the plane as a military weapon, it helped to establish aviation, train pilots, foster aircraft manufacturing and increase the public's awareness of aviation's possibilities.

Many men took to flying. They bought surplus Government airplanes, and earned their living doing stunt flying and taking people up for short flights around airports. These men were the so-called "gypsies" and "barnstormers" who helped aviation to grow.

Glenn Curtis was not only a plane designer and pilot, but also a manufacturer.

The NC-4 proved, 1919, that a v ocean expanse co not limit travel by

In May 1919, the NC-4 made aviation

How did airplanes "shrink" the world?

history by crossing the Atlantic. The Navy had three patrol bombers, flying boats which could take off and land only in water. Each plane carried a crew of six. Only the NC-4 completed the journey from Rockaway, Long Island to Plymouth, England, a distance of 3,925 miles. Some fifty destroyers lined the Atlantic to act as guides for the planes and to be ready to help any that were in distress. The total flying time was 52½ hours, not including the time necessary at the seven stops for refueling and repairs.

In 1924, the Army sent its Douglas biplane bombers on a flight around the world. Four planes left Seattle, Washington on April 6. On September 28, only two — the *Chicago* and the *New Orleans* — returned. They had crossed twenty-eight countries, covered 26,345

Some 33 hours and 30 minutes after he took off from Roosevelt Field in Long Island, Lindbergh landed his *Spirit of St. Louis* at Le Bourget, an airfield outside of Paris.

Two Douglas World Cruisers carried their Army flight crews in the first round-the-world flight in 1924.

During parts of their trip, the landing wheels were replaced by pontoons.

miles, and crossed the Pacific for the first time. The actual flying time was about 15½ days.

The race from New York to Paris was

Who made the first nonstop solo flight across the Atlantic?

spurred by a $25,000 prize which Raymond Orteig, French-born owner of a New York hotel, offered to the first one to make the flight nonstop. Although Orteig offered this money in 1919, it was not until 1926 that Rene Founck, a famous French aviator of World War I, made the first try. His plane crashed at take-off.

Many others tried and failed. It was Captain Charles A. Lindbergh, a former mail pilot, Army officer and barnstormer, who finally claimed the prize. Financed by a group of St. Louis businessmen, Lindbergh had Ryan Aircraft of San Diego build a special monoplane with a Wright J-5 Whirlwind engine at a cost of $10,580. The builders at Ryan worked as many as eighteen hours a day to complete the plane in sixty days.

Lindbergh brought his plane, *The Spirit of St. Louis,* to Roosevelt Field, Long Island where, despite the fog and drizzle, he took off at 7:52 A.M. on May 20, 1927. To make room for extra gasoline, Lindbergh flew alone. To make the plane lighter, he carried no parachute and removed the radio and all other "surplus" equipment and charts.

Alone, with no radio, Lindbergh plowed through rain, sleet, fog and high winds across the Atlantic, flew over Ireland and England and on over France. He circled the Eiffel Tower and landed nearby at the airport of Le Bourget, on May 21 at 10:22 P.M., Paris time. He had flown over 3,600 miles in 33 hours and 30 minutes.

The "Lone Eagle," as Lindbergh was called, was greeted by large, enthusiastic crowds. He received wild welcomes everywhere he went. The world was talking about "Lucky Lindy" — and aviation.

FAMOUS FIRSTS IN EARLY AVIATION

The first air-mail service was established by the U. S. Post Office between New York and Washington, D. C. on May 15, 1918. Major Reuben Fleet piloted the first flight and Lieutenant George Boyle made the return flight.

* * *

The first nonstop transatlantic flight was made by Captain John Alcock and Lieutenant Arthur Whitten Brown of England in a Vickers-Vimy biplane on June 14, 1919. They flew from Newfoundland to Clifden, Ireland, in 16 hours and 12 minutes.

* * *

The first nonstop transcontinental flight from New York to San Diego was made by Lieutenants Oakley Kelly and John Macready in May, 1923. Their trip in a Fokker T-2 took 26 hours and 50 minutes.

* * *

The first airplane flight over the North Pole was made on May 9, 1926. Lieutenant Floyd Bennett piloted a trimotor Fokker, commanded by Commander Richard E. Byrd, from Spitzbergen, Norway. During the 15 hours, before the plane returned to its base, it flew over the Pole.

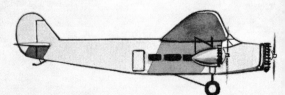

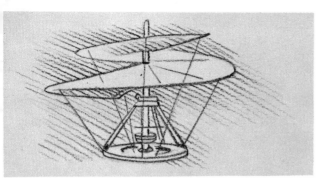

Da Vinci designed a helixpteron, the first helicopter.

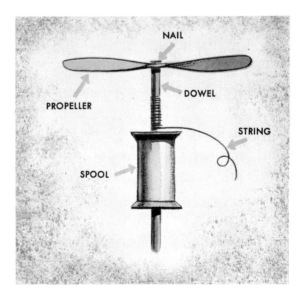

The Launoy, or Chinese flying top, was the first successful model of a heavier-than-air machine that man built. It was the basis for the development of copters.

Flying in Any Direction

A helicopter can fly in any direction — straight up, straight down, forward, backward, sideways — and it can even stand still in mid-air. Furthermore, the helicopter can creep along a few inches above the ground or water, or it can climb thousands of feet into the sky and travel at over 100 miles per hour.

The fifteenth century genius, Leonardo **How did the helicopter originate?** da Vinci, not only designed a workable parachute and the ornithopter, but he also designed a very special flying machine. Overhead, it had a large screw-shaped propeller, which da Vinci hoped would screw into the air and lift the machine. He called this flying machine the *helixpteron* (hel-i-TER-on), which comes from the Greek *helix* (meaning "spiral") and *pteron* (meaning "wing").

For more than two hundred fifty years no one paid attention to this idea. But in 1783, the French naturalist Launoy "discovered" a Chinese flying top, a toy probably brought back from the Orient. The top was made of feathers, wood and string and it could fly straight up. It was the first man-made heavier-than-air object that could leave the ground on its own power.

This top inspired George Cayley and he built a similar one, but used tin for the blades instead of feathers. The Cayley top rose 90 feet into the air.

All you need in order to make a Cayley **How can you make a Cayley top?** top is a 6-inch model airplane propeller, an empty spool, a dowel that just about slides through the hole in the spool and a piece of string about 2 feet long.

Nail the propeller to one end of the dowel. Wind the string around the

21

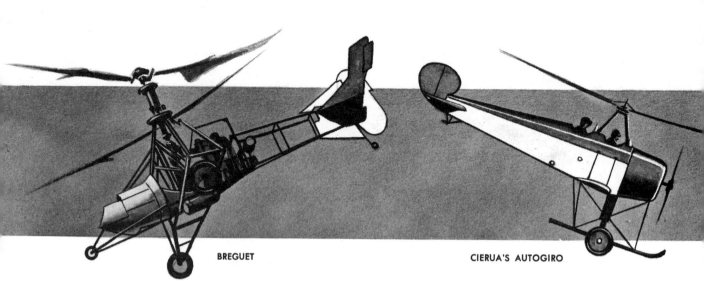

BREGUET

CIERUA'S AUTOGIRO

dowel, about an inch below the propeller. Then, slide the dowel into the spool. Hold the spool in one hand with the propeller pointing straight up. Pull the string hard and quickly with the other hand. The propeller spins and lifts the dowel straight into the air.

In 1878, Enrico Forlanini, using a powerful, tiny steam engine he designed and built, made a model helicopter. This steam-driven model hovered in the air at about 40 feet for 20 seconds. It provided positive proof that such a flying machine was possible.

Who were the early helicopter builders?

The first full-sized helicopter to fly was built by Louis Breguet in 1907. This plane rose some 5 feet off the ground, but it could not be controlled and was unstable. It was not until 1922 that Russian-born George de Bothezat built and flew a helicopter that was stable and controllable. His *Flying Octopus,* built as a military helicopter, was an enormous ship with four rotors or horizontal blades. Although it made over one hundred successful flights from McCook Field in the United States, it

was abandoned because it was too clumsy and complicated.

The *autogyro* (auto-GY-ro) is a hybrid, a combination of an airplane and helicopter. Its Spanish inventor, Juan de la Cierva, used a small biplane and attached a set of whirling blades on top of the plane. There was no engine to work the top blades. They turned as the air from the propeller rushed passed them.

How does an autogyro fly?

The turning of the rotary blades gave the plane extra lift or upward pull. For this reason, it was possible for the plane to take off at a slower engine speed and get into the air in less time. It appeared to jump into the air at take-off.

The autogyro's whirling blades turned only when the plane's propeller was spinning and, therefore, it hovered in the air. The only advantage of the autogyro was its ability to get into the air quickly at a lower engine speed. Although the autogyro has disappeared from the sky, the development of flexible rotary blades by Juan de la Cierva helped make it possible to build truly successful helicopters.

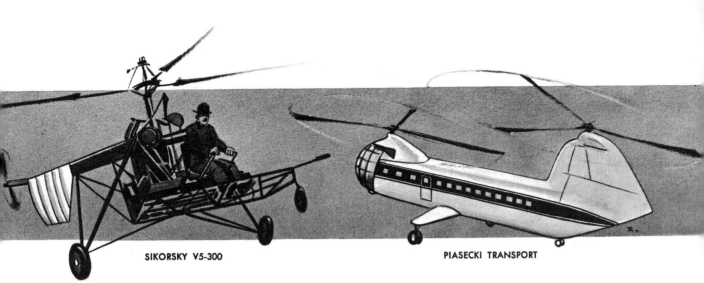

SIKORSKY V5-300

PIASECKI TRANSPORT

One man stands out in the history of helicopters — Igor Sikorsky. As a young man in Kiev, Russia, he built a model helicopter in 1910. He continued to study the experiments of others and in 1939, working in the United States, he decided to try again.

Who perfected the helicopter?

For months, he worked on "Igor's Nightmare," as many people called his helicopter. He conducted many experiments and in May, 1940, he tried his first free flight. It was an overwhelming success compared with anything that preceded it. His ship could fly up, down, backward, sideways, and could hover in the air. But his ship had difficulty in flying forward. Additional work solved this problem and he started to produce workable helicopters.

World War II spurred the development of helicopters and in 1943, eighteen-year-old Stanley Hiller, Jr. designed and built the first coaxial helicopter. He used one engine to turn both rotors.

The helicopter is used to spray chemicals over crops to protect them from insects, to fight forest fires, to carry mail, to inspect power lines and pipe lines in rugged mountain country. It is also used in land- and sea-rescue work, by cowboys on very large ranches, and even acts as a "bus" between airports.

The rotor blades over the helicopter lift the ship and make it fly. The blades act somewhat like the wings of an airplane. The pilot of a helicopter can tilt these blades — this tilt is called *pitch*. Tilting the moving blades creates lift. If you have ever flown a kite, you know how this works.

How does the helicopter fly?

To climb into the air, the pilot tilts the moving blades and the helicopter goes straight up. When he wants to come down, he decreases the tilt, or pitch, of the blades. This decreases the lift, and gravity brings the ship down. If he wants to hover or stand still in the air, he sets the pitch of the blades so that the upward lift equals the pull toward the ground. Now, picture these moving blades as a saucer. You can tilt the entire saucer in any direction. It is through this tilting that the pilot can make the plane go forward, backward or sideways.

Near the tail of the helicopter is a smaller set of blades which revolve. By controlling their pitch, the pilot can keep the ship straight or make right and left turns.

A miniature helicopter is capable of

How do the modern ornithopters fly?

carrying one man. He can fly straight up, sideways, forward, backward, downward, or hover in the air. The personal *whirlywings* have been used experimentally by the U. S. Army for its scouts.

The *aerocycle,* another version of a one-man helicopter used by the Army, is somewhat larger than a *whirlywing* and the man stands on top of the cycle to fly it through the air.

This is a U. S. Army craft — a whirlywing.

Another small, one-man flying machine is the *flying platform*. It is shaped like a large doughnut and has a fan in the center. This fan lifts and propels the platform on which the man stands. The pilot's "leaning" controls the horizontal flight of this craft.

Air Cushion Vehicles (ACV's) are related-type hovering craft which move about suspended above a surface on a "cushion" of air. This cushion is formed by blowing a large volume of air down beneath the vehicle, using a fan, and

FLYING PLATFORM

holding it in place by a flexible skirt around the vehicle's outer edge. Propellers mounted in the ACV propel it at high speed.

Picture an airplane, higher than a three-

What is VTOL?

story building, standing on its tail. The propeller starts turning and soon the plane goes straight up into the air. Once the

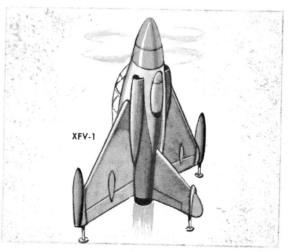

XFV-1

pilot gets up as high as he wants to go, he maneuvers the plane to a horizontal position and it flies like any ordinary airplane. Such planes, often called "flying pogo sticks," are VTOL aircraft. VTOL means "vertical take-off and landing." They can take off from land or any surface.

Not only can these planes take off and land vertically, but they can hover in the air as well. Also, they fly at speeds up to 500 miles per hour. Some VTOL aircraft are powered by rotors which tilt upward for takeoff and landing and tilt forward for horizontal flight. Some others have fans built into the wings which force air downward for vertical liftoff. Propellers or jet engines propel these aircraft forward.

Theory and Facts of Flight

About forty years before the American

Why does an airplane fly?

Revolution, a Swiss scientist, Daniel Bernoulli, discovered that in any moving fluid the pressure is lowest where the speed is greatest. If we can increase the speed of air above a surface, such as a wing, pressure should decrease. The wing should rise.

In actual practice, the wing of an airplane is shaped somewhat like a bow — the upper surface is curved while the lower part is straight. Since the air has to travel a greater distance over the top part of the wing, it must travel at a greater speed. As a result, the pressure is lower above the wing than below it and the wing rises, or *lifts,* into the air. Engineers are constantly improving the shape of airplane wings for greater lift.

When an airplane flies horizontally, its propulsion system — a propeller or jet engine — must do two things. It must overcome the friction of the air in order to pull the plane forward, and it must move the plane fast enough forward to increase the speed of the air over the wings to create lift. Lift is the upward pressure on the wing. Lift overcomes *gravity* — the downward pressure created by the weight of the plane.

A propeller slices through the air in the same way that a screw cuts into wood, and pulls the plane forward. This forward motion of the propeller is called *thrust.* It counteracts the *drag* of the atmosphere, the force that resists forward motion.

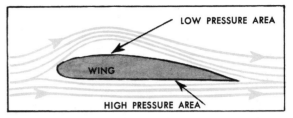

As the air rushes past the wing, or airfoil, it flows above and below the airfoil. The shape of the airfoil causes the air to travel a greater distance over the top of the foil. This results in a lowering of air pressure, which creates an upward lift on the airfoil.

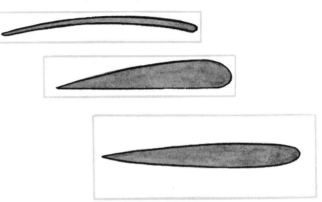

Airfoil cross sections, top to bottom: Design used by Wright brothers; "high-light" wing used on small planes; "high-speed" wing used by commercial liners. Improved wing designs result in higher speeds and smoother flights.

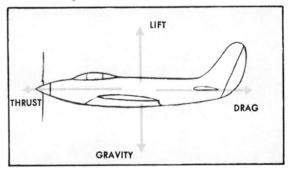

These four forces act upon a plane while in flight.

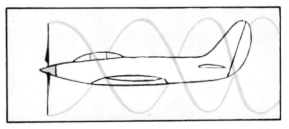

The propeller, called airscrews in England, provides the forward pulling or lifting power of an airplane.

An airplane, like any moving object

What makes an airplane go up and down? following the basic laws of physics, tends to continue in a straight line unless some force is exerted to change its direction. The speed at which the engine turns the propeller is governed by the *throttle*. Opening the throttle increases the air speed and lifts the plane higher.

Equally important is the *elevator* which controls the plane's upward and downward movement. It is a horizontal, hinged surface attached to the tail. When the pilot applies back pressure on the control stick, or column, the elevator is tilted upward. The air, striking the raised elevator, forces the tail down and the wing upward. The thrust of the propeller pulls the plane upward. Conversely, when the pilot pushes the control stick forward, the elevator is tilted downward. This forces the tail up and the wing down.

Two parts of an airplane control its

How does an airplane turn? turns to the right and left. The *rudder*, a vertical surface that is hinged to the tail, swings the tail to the right or left just in the same way as a section of the tail swings up or down. On the ground, it is used to make the plane turn just as a rudder of a boat does. In the air, however, the major purpose of the rudder is *not* to make the plane turn, but to assist the plane in entering and recovering from a turn.

The *ailerons,* small sections of the rear edge of the wing, near the tips, are hinged and are so connected that as one rises, the other lowers. This action tends to raise one wing and lower the other.

When the aileron on the right wing is lowered, the right wing rises and the plane will be tilted, or *banked,* to the left. The lifting force on the right wing is no longer completely upward — part of the force is pulling the plane to the left. This, in combination with the rudder, produces a left turn; that is, the plane is "lifted" around the turn.

The propeller provides the power for the forward thrust. The elevators enable the pilot to make the plane go up or down. The flaps aid in the ascent and help provide a smoother descent. The ailerons and rudder help the plane to turn left and right.

AILERON
FLAP
VERTICAL STABILIZER
ELEVATOR
RUDDER
FUSELAGE
ELEVATOR
ENGINE COWL
HORIZONTAL STABILIZER
FLAP
AILERON
PROPELLER
WING STRUT
WING
LANDING GEAR

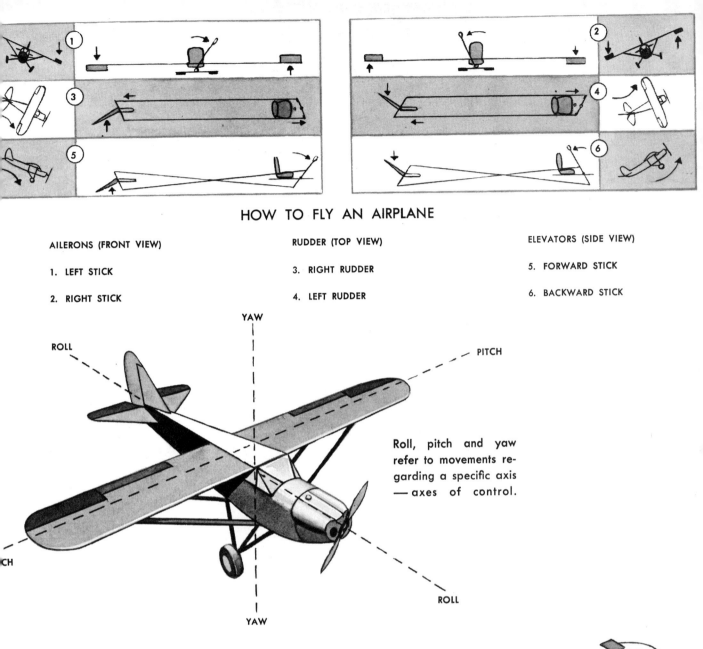

HOW TO FLY AN AIRPLANE

AILERONS (FRONT VIEW)	RUDDER (TOP VIEW)	ELEVATORS (SIDE VIEW)
1. LEFT STICK	3. RIGHT RUDDER	5. FORWARD STICK
2. RIGHT STICK	4. LEFT RUDDER	6. BACKWARD STICK

Roll, pitch and yaw refer to movements regarding a specific axis — axes of control.

How can you demonstrate *lift*?

Take a piece of paper about 2 inches wide and about 5 inches long. Fold it an inch from the end. Hold the paper with your forefinger and thumb so that the fold is about an inch or two from your mouth. Blow with all your might over the top of the paper.

What happened? The paper moves up or *lifts*. By increasing the speed of the air over the top of the paper, you have reduced the pressure, causing the paper to rise.

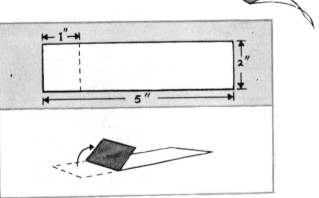

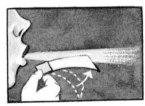

You can demonstrate lift, caused by the Bernoulli effect, on the upper surface of a piece of paper (right).

27

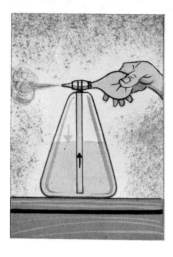

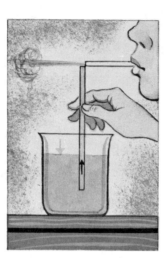

You can demonstrate this same principle with a simple atomizer. Blowing across the top of the tube — you can use a straw — reduces the pressure and causes the liquid to rise within the tube.

Take a 3 by 5 index card and fold a 1-inch section along the long edge upward at a 45-degree angle. Paste the card, along its short center line, to a piece of balsa wood

How can you demonstrate the working of an elevator?

about 10 inches long. Balance the wood with the attached card on a round pencil, like a seesaw. Mark this "balance" point and push a straight pin through the balsa so that it is parallel to the card.

Hold the pin lightly between the thumb and forefinger of both hands. Hold the balsa wood in front of your mouth with the card farthest away. Now when you blow with all your might, the raised portion of the index card acts like a plane's elevator. The front end of the balsa wood (nearest your mouth) will move upward, like the nose of a plane.

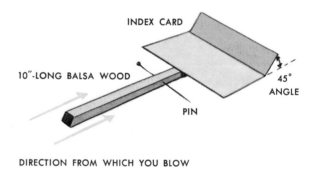

INDEX CARD

10"-LONG BALSA WOOD

45° ANGLE

PIN

DIRECTION FROM WHICH YOU BLOW

WHAT DO THE INSTRUMENTS TELL THE PILOT?

Here are only a few of the more important instruments which a pilot uses to guide his airplane:

Oil Pressure Gauge indicates the pressure of the oil in the engine. The dial is colored so that it is easier for the pilot to instantly spot any danger.

Oil Temperature Gauge tells the temperature of the oil in the engine.

Rate-of-Climb Indicator tells the pilot the speed at which his plane is climbing

or dropping. The indicator is at zero when the plane is flying level.

Air Speed Indicator notes how fast the plane is moving through the air. Four colors are used for greater safety. Red is used to show maximum speed at which the plane can fly. Yellow shows a caution range — speeds approaching maximum speed. Heavy blue is used for normal cruising speeds. Light blue is used to show landing speed.

Turn-and-Bank Indicator is actually two separate instruments. The curved glass tube with a metal ball in liquid, the bank indicator, located near the bottom of the instrument, shows whether the plane is tilted to the right or left. The turn indicator shows the direction in which the nose of the plane is headed — to the left, straight ahead or to the right.

Instrument Landing System Indicator helps the pilot land his plane when the airfield is covered by fog or very low clouds. When the two pointers line up with the white circles on the dial, the plane is directly on path approaching the runway for a perfect landing.

Fuel Gauge indicates how much gasoline the plane has in its tank.

Tachometer tells the pilot how his motor is doing. It indicates the number of revolutions of the engine or the speed at which the propellers are turning.

Altimeter shows the height of the plane above the ground. There are three pointers — the smallest shows height in tens of thousands of feet above the ground; the medium-sized pointer shows height in thousands of feet; and the longest pointer shows height in hundreds and parts of hundreds of feet. The altimeter pictured here shows an altitude, or height, of 14,750 feet.

OIL PRESSURE GAUGE

OIL TEMPERATURE GAUGE

RATE-OF-CLIMB INDICATOR

AIR SPEED INDICATOR

TURN-AND-BANK INDICATOR

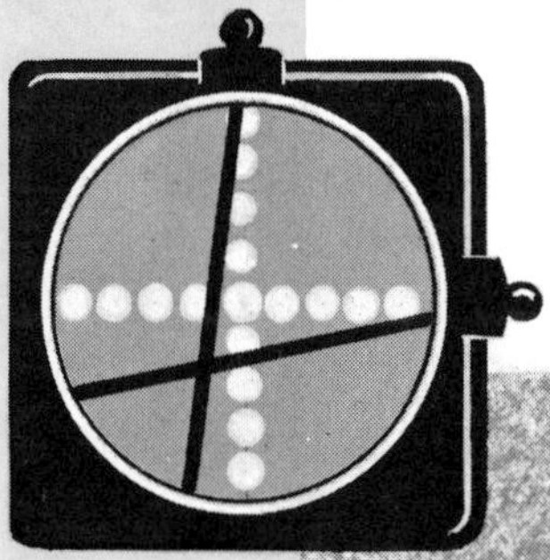

INSTRUMENT LANDING SYSTEM INDICATOR

ALTIMETER

TACHOMETER

FUEL GAUGE

Directional Gyro and Magnetic Compass are used to guide the plane. The magnetic compass acts like any regular compass you have seen — it points to the north. The directional gyro is used by the pilot to set his course. If the plane changes direction, the gyro shows this to the pilot.

Artificial Horizon helps a pilot when he is flying at night, in a cloud or in fog. During a clear day, a pilot keeps his plane straight and level by watching the horizon. At other times, he must use this instrument.

Drift Indicator is usually installed level with the floor. It shows the pilot how the wind might be blowing him off course.

In multi-engine, conventional aircraft, there is a separate oil pressure and oil temperature indicator and a tachometer for each engine. In addition, there is generally a separate fuel gauge for each tank in the plane. Thus, if you were to look at the panel of a large four-engine airliner which has six fuel tanks, you would see seventeen more instruments than you see here. Furthermore, there is an identical set of dials for the co-pilot in addition to the pilot, and on some planes a third set of dials is used for the navigator-engineer.

Highways of the Air

There are thousands of airports of many different kinds throughout the world. In the United States, the Federal Aviation Administration (FAA) classifies the airports according to the length of their runways. An airport with a runway of 1,500 to 2,300 feet is classified as a personal airport and is used only by small, light, private planes.

DIRECTIONAL GYRO AND
MAGNETIC COMPASS

ARTIFICIAL HORIZON

DRIFT INDICATOR

Airports range from the small grass fields for two- and four-passen-

ger planes to the very large fields with concrete runways that handle the large commercial jet airliners.

Airports where large domestic passenger airliners can land and take off must have runways of 6,000 to 7,000 feet. To meet the needs of today's large jetliners, some airports have runways of 10,000 feet or more, or about two miles.

In the air between the airports are **What are the airways?** *airways,* or roads, through the sky along which the planes travel. Because of the many planes flying overhead, both during the day and night, it is necessary to set up rules for the road just as we have traffic rules for the cars on the streets.

Except when taking off or landing, airplanes must fly at least 500 feet above the ground. Over cities and other congested areas, the planes are required to fly 1,000 or even 2,000 feet above the ground.

The route a plane takes is determined by the FAA which controls all air traffic. At major airports, there are men sitting before air maps, radios and control boards, and they keep track of every plane as it plows through the skies.

Specific airways have been established to prevent planes from colliding in the air. All eastbound flights — planes flying from west to east — fly at *odd* thousand-foot levels, plus 500 feet, above sea level. Thus, a plane flying from Los Angeles to New York could fly at 15,500 feet. Westbound flights, on the other hand, fly at *even* thousand-foot levels, plus 500 feet, above sea level.

31

WHICH PLANE HAS THE RIGHT OF WAY?

Aircraft have rules that govern the right of way in the sky.

All flying craft have to give the right of way to a balloon.

Airplanes and airships have to give a glider the right of way.

An airplane must give an airship the right of way.

*   *   *

If two planes are flying so that their paths might cross, the plane to the right of the pilot has the right of way.

*   *   *

Should two planes be approaching head-on, both pilots must shift their planes to the right. As they pass, the planes must be at least 500 feet apart.

The same plane going from New York to Los Angeles could fly at 14,500 feet.

During a clear, sunny day — or Class C **How do air markers help pilots to fly?** weather according to the Air Weather Bureau — planes can fly by contact; that is, the pilot can see the ground and identify his route. There are various markers along the route on the ground. These markers also appear on special flight maps which the pilot carries with him just as we carry a road map in a car.

The air markers indicate location, have arrows pointing to the nearest airport and other identifying information. The markers are painted on highways, roofs of barns and factories, and the sides of high buildings such as grain elevators. They are also set in stone on mountains or in fields.

In addition to the visible markers, there is also radio contact. The CAA operates many radio stations throughout the country. By picking up different stations, the pilot can determine his exact position over the ground.

During the night, when it is clear, the pilot can spot visible ground markers, some of which are illuminated, special air beacons (similar to lights from a lighthouse) and airport lights and beacons.

Look into the cockpit of an airplane **How do pilots fly in all types of weather?** and you will see a maze of dials, knobs, switches and levers. These instruments and controls help the pilot at take-off, when he guides the plane safely through the airways and when he lands. Today's plane can land even when the pilot cannot see the airport.

The Instrument Landing System (ILS) is used when the airport's *ceiling* (the height from the ground to the clouds above) is too low for the pilot to land by sight. Through the use of electronic equipment, the pilot can "see" through the fog, rain, sleet and dark. A special instrument on his flight panel helps him align his airplane directly with the airport's runway. The instrument also shows him if he is too high or too low as he approaches.

Radar is also used to help pilots fly

through foul weather and to land safely. The major airports use Air Surveillance Radar (ASR) with which they can pinpoint the exact position in the sky of any plane within 60 miles of the airport. Some of the newer *blind landing* techniques (when the pilot cannot see the airport landing strip) involve automatic controls. The pilot sets the plane on special electronic instruments, and a ground controller, using radar, actually lands the plane.

Faster Than Sound

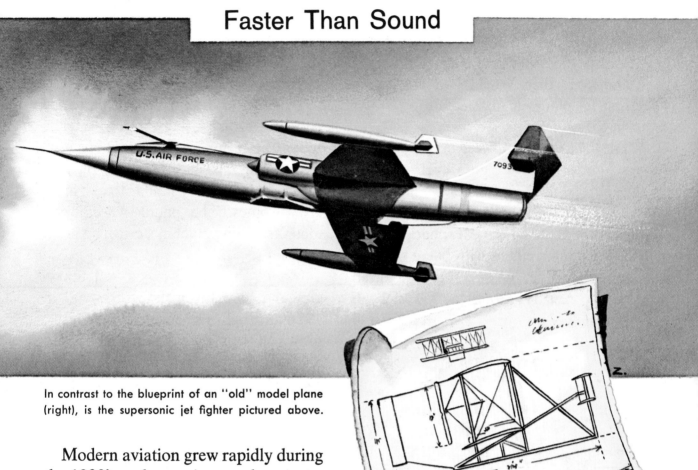

In contrast to the blueprint of an "old" model plane (right), is the supersonic jet fighter pictured above.

Modern aviation grew rapidly during the 1930's and new air records were established. In mid-1931, Wiley Post and Harold Gatty winged their way around the world in 8 days, 15 hours and 51 minutes. Two years later, Wiley Post set out by himself in his plane, the *Winnie Mae,* and made the same earth-circling trip in 7 days, 8 hours and 49 minutes. During this flight, he used two new aviation instruments — the radio compass and a robot or automatic pilot.

It has been said that the world was put on wings when the Douglas DC-3 was introduced in 1936. Until that time, the airlines used small planes, such as the Fokker trimotor and Ford trimotor. Each carried only eight people and reached top speeds of about 100 miles an hour. The DC-3 carried twenty-one passengers in addition to a crew of three, and it could fly at 180 miles per hour. This "workhorse of the airlines" helped to build air passenger travel in the United States.

The outbreak of World War II in September, 1939 signaled a new era in aviation history. Emphasis was placed on faster fighter planes, on larger bombers that could fly higher, and on troop transports that could carry more men and fly farther. World War II saw the first jet planes in real action.

The idea of jet power, or propulsion,

When were jets first used?

goes back to early history. The Greek mathematician, Hero, who lived in Alexandria about 130 B.C., is credited with being the first to build a jet engine. He converted steam pressure into jet action with an "engine" of his own design. It consisted

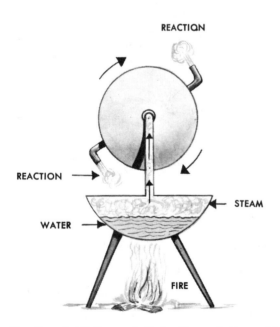

The "aeoliphile" was built by Hero of Alexandria.

of a hollow metal sphere which was mounted so that it could spin freely. The steam inside the sphere escaped through small nozzles, causing the sphere to spin. This engine was a scientific toy and was never put to use.

The jet principle was put to work during the Middle Ages in Europe. The *smoke-jack,* which some claim da Vinci invented, was used to turn a roasting spit in a fireplace. The turning action of the spit was produced by a fan in the chimney. The hot air passing up the chimney turned the fan.

In 1629, Giovanni Branca perfected a steam turbine using the jet principle to operate a milling machine. He used steam, which passed through a pipe, to turn a paddle-wheel similar to our modern turbines. The paddle-wheel operated the milling machine, crushing grain into flour.

Many other men worked on jet-powered machines over the years, and in 1926 an English scientist, Dr. Griffiths, proposed the use of jet-powered gas turbines to power an airplane. The first successful jet-plane flight was made in Germany when a Heinkel He-178 took to the air on August 27, 1939.

Have you ever pressed a spring together

How does a jet fly?

and let it go? What happens? It springs back to its original size. The air around us behaves in the same way. When you compress air, it tries to escape and expand to its original volume. When you heat air, it expands, and also tries to escape. Compressing and heating air give the jet engine its power.

If you take an inflated balloon and let it go, the air inside the balloon will escape. As it rushes out, the balloon "flies" through the air. This illustrates the principle which makes the jet fly. It is an example of Newton's third law of motion: "For every action, there is an equal and opposite reaction." As the air rushes out the back, the balloon goes forward.

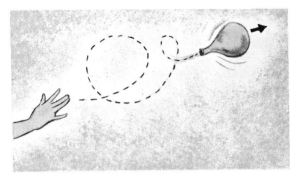

The balloon's activity is a form of jet propulsion.

There are several types of jet engines and all work on the same principle. A jet plane needs no propeller since it uses air to give it forward motion or thrust. The most common type of jet engine is the turbojet.

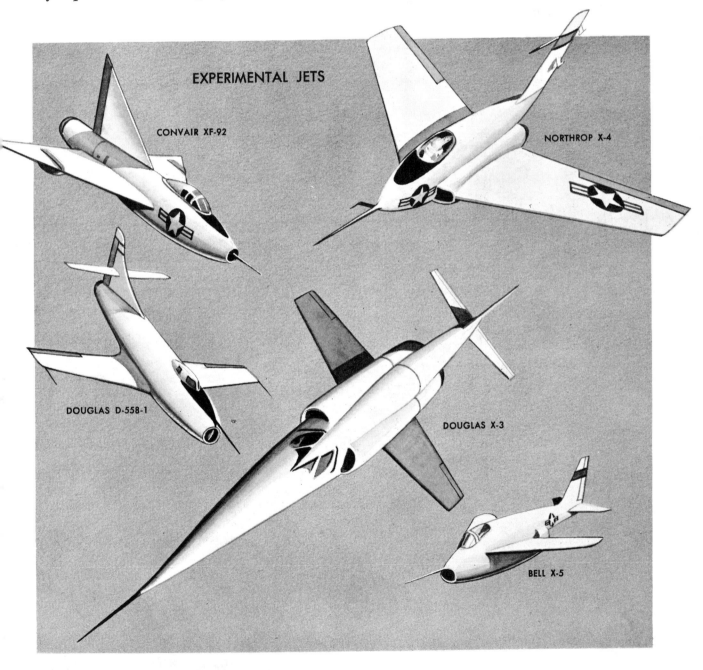

EXPERIMENTAL JETS

CONVAIR XF-92

NORTHROP X-4

DOUGLAS D-558-1

DOUGLAS X-3

BELL X-5

RAMJET AND PULSEJET

The *ramjet* is the simplest of all jet engines. It has no moving parts. The air is compressed by the forward motion of the plane. The plane has to be in motion *before* the ramjet works. Therefore, a plane with a ramjet engine has to be launched in the air by a "mother ship."

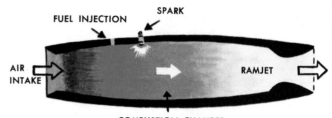

The *pulsejet* is also a simple jet engine. It has only one moving part, an inlet valve which controls the amount of air entering the engine. It was first used during World War II to power the V-1 flying bombs which the Germans rocketed into London, England.

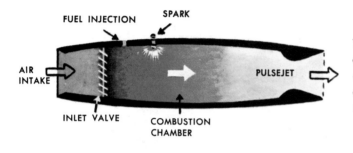

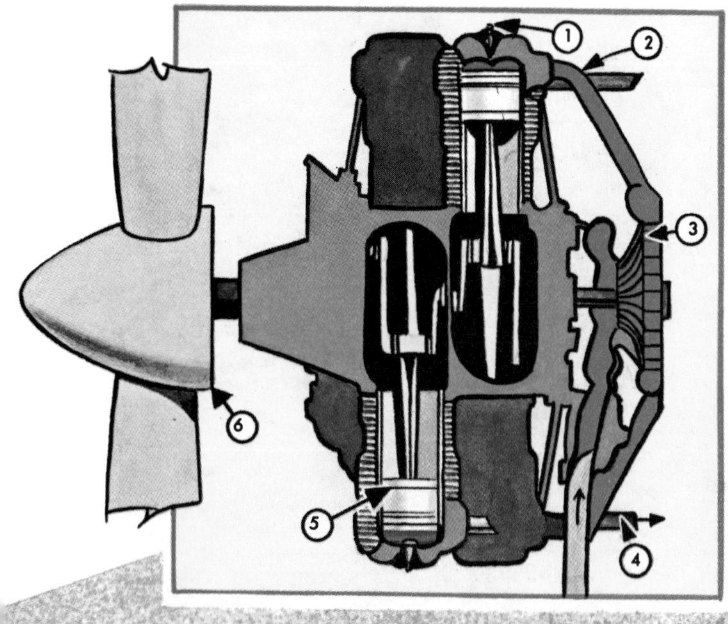

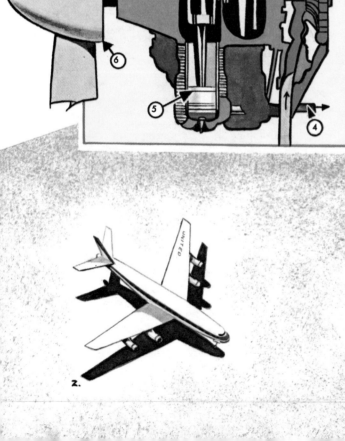

A reciprocating engine: (1) spark plug; (2) cylinder inlet; (3) shaft-driven supercharger; (4) cylinder exhaust; (5) piston; and (6) propeller.

Super aircraft require special aircraft facilities. Shown below is a typically modern structure which handles traffic at John F. Kennedy International Airport.

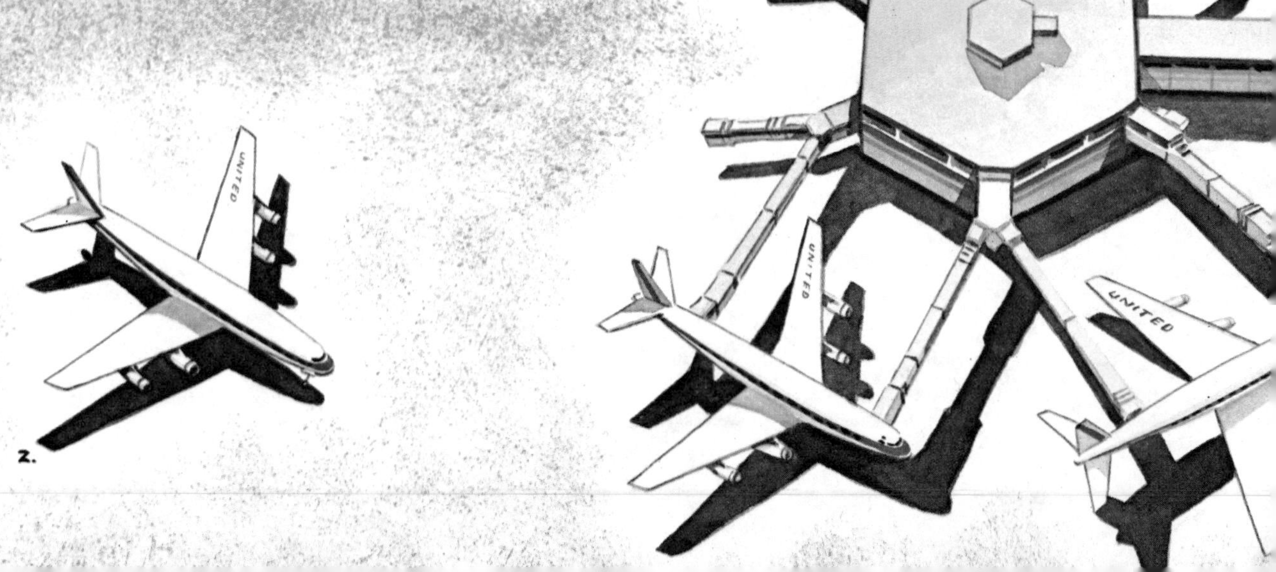

2.

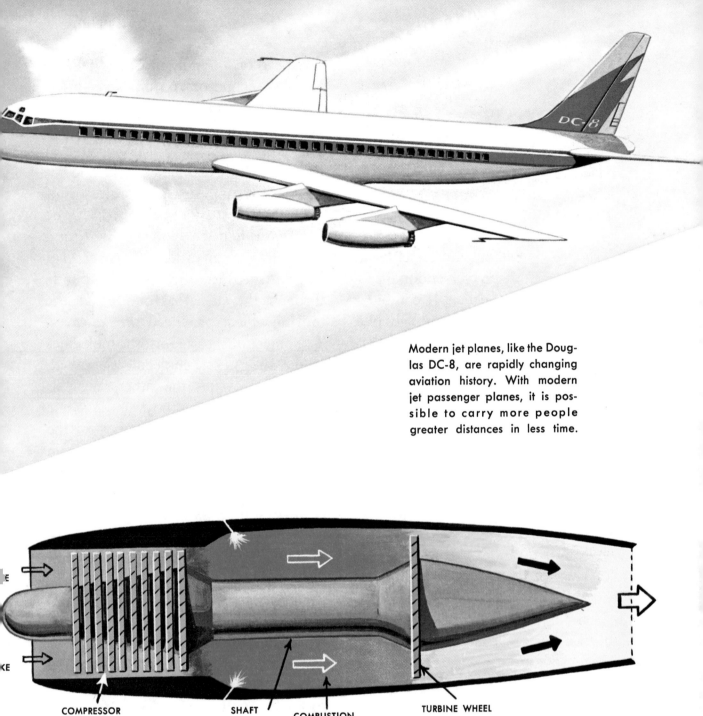

Modern jet planes, like the Douglas DC-8, are rapidly changing aviation history. With modern jet passenger planes, it is possible to carry more people greater distances in less time.

COMPRESSOR SHAFT COMBUSTION CHAMBER TURBINE WHEEL

HOW A TURBOJET WORKS

1. Air is sucked into the engine through the front intake. The compressor, acting like a large fan, compresses the air and forces it through ducts, or tubes, to the combustion chamber.

2. In the combustion chamber, fuel is sprayed into the compressed air and ignited. The resulting hot gases expand rapidly and, with terrific force, blast their way out of the rear of the engine. This jet blast gives the engine and plane its forward thrust.

3. As the hot gases rush out of the engine, they pass through a set of blades, the turbine wheel. These blades react like a windmill and turn the main engine shaft, which operates the front compressor.

4. Some engines, designed to give extra pushing power, have an afterburner attached to the engine. This is a long tail cone in which more fuel is sprayed and burned, just before the gases pass through the rear exhaust.

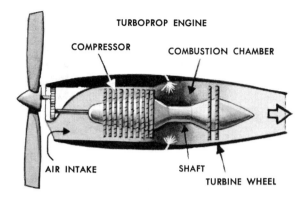

TURBOPROP ENGINE

COMPRESSOR — COMBUSTION CHAMBER

AIR INTAKE — SHAFT — TURBINE WHEEL

A *turboprop* is a jet engine connected to

Why do they use turboprops?

a conventional propeller. It combines the advantages of a gas turbine jet with those of a propeller. During take-off and low speeds, the propeller produces higher forward thrust. During landing, the propeller creates greater drag, enabling the plane to take off and land in shorter distances than a turbojet. However, the gas turbine jet is lightweight as compared with a conventional plane's piston motor and is without vibration in flight.

A turboprop, or *propjet* as it is also called, cannot fly as fast or as high as a turbojet. Turbojets are particularly suited for high-speed and high-altitude flights. On the other hand, propjets are more efficient at moderate altitudes than conventional piston-engine planes.

Have you ever noticed that during a

What is the sound barrier?

lightning storm you can see the flash of lightning before you hear the thunder? This is because light travels faster than sound. The speed of sound in freezing air (32°F.) is about 1,090 feet per second or 743 miles per hour. The speed of sound increases as the temperature rises, about a foot a second faster for each degree. At 68°F.,

the speed of sound in air is about 1,130 feet per second or 765 miles per hour.

Sound travels through the air in waves similar to those produced when you drop a stone into a pond. One of the people who studied sound and air waves was an Austrian professor of physics, Ernest Mach. About 1870, he photographed cannon shells flying through the air in order to discover what happens to an object as it speeds through the air. He found that the moving object produced *shock waves*. The object pushes against the molecules in the air. As one molecule is pushed, it in turn pushes the others near it. Imagine a long line of boys standing one behind the other. The last boy in the line gets pushed. As he moves forward, he pushes the boy in front of him. This happens all the way down the line. This is how sound and shock waves are produced.

As the speed of a plane approaches the speed of sound, it is pushing rapidly against the molecules in the air and creating shock waves. As the plane reaches the same speed as sound, these waves pile up and form an invisible barrier. When the plane exceeds the speed of sound, it must "crash" through

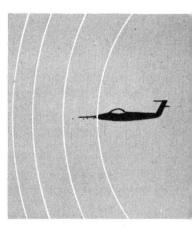

As the plane goes through the air, it creates sound waves. The plane itself displaces air about it as it speeds forward.

this barrier. As it does, it creates a thunderlike sound. You will see the plane before you hear its motor, just as you see lightning before you hear the thunder.

As planes began to fly higher and faster,

How did the sound barrier change the shape of planes? the planes vibrated fiercely and the pilots had difficulty operating the controls. These pilots had encountered *wave drag,* the piling-up of air in front of the plane. Scientists and airmen studied this effect on planes and soon recognized what was happening.

To honor the man who first explored this subject scientifically, we measure the speed of a plane or rocket in *Mach numbers.* Aeronautical engineers use Mach 1 as equal to 680 miles per hour, the speed of sound at about 35,000 feet and higher, where the temperature is 50° or lower. Mach 2 equals twice the speed of sound or 1,360 miles per hour.

They found that the shock waves which caused wave drag were shaped like a cone. If the plane has long wings, it tends to spin more easily. As a result, jet planes, designed to fly faster than sound, have shorter wings set farther

back along the sides of the body. These wings sweep back from the sides of the airplane to conform to the shape of the shock wave. This increases the speed of the airplane and makes it more stable.

Scientists have studied sound waves and plane speeds in special wind tunnels using model planes, and thus, have helped engineers to develop better planes.

As planes climbed higher in to the air,

Why do planes fly in the jet stream? meteorologists (weathermen) and pilots discovered fast-moving "rivers of air" above the earth. These rivers generally flow in an east-west direction and reach speeds of almost 300 miles per hour. The fast-moving "rivers" are called *jet streams* because jet aircraft

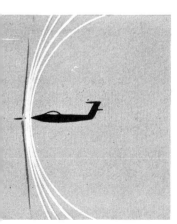

As the plane's speed is increased, approaching at the speed of sound, it is increasing the compression of the sound waves.

As the speed of the plane exceeds that of the waves it created, it then plunges headlong through the sound barrier.

often enter them to be pushed along.

A plane flying in the same direction as a jet stream is pushed along in the same way you are pushed by a strong wind when you are walking in the same direction as the wind is blowing. A plane flying 600 miles per hour in a jet stream moving 300 miles per hour is actually traveling 900 miles an hour over the earth. Flying in the jet stream shortens flying time and conserves fuel.

An SST is a *supersonic transport*, an

What is an SST? airliner that flies faster than the speed of sound. The first SST was built by France and England, working together. In 1978 it carried 120 passengers from New York to London in 2½ hours, at a speed of 1,320 miles per hour. About two years later the Soviet Union also built an SST.

Now, almost nine years after the first flight of an SST, the French-English company flies supersonic planes to almost all parts of the Western world. Flying a transport plane at twice the speed of sound uses very much fuel and requires special jet engines. Fares on an SST are very high.

As jet engines became more and

What will future planes be like? more powerful, more passengers and heavier loads could be carried. Today some airliners carry more than 300 passengers. Cargo planes such as the Air Force's *Galaxy* carry loads of 125 tons.

In the future, for long flights, a plane will take off from an airport, using jet engines. It will rise into the stratosphere, where rocket engines will push it into outer space. With no air drag to combat, the rockets will accelerate the plane to very high speed, then shut off. The plane, now perhaps halfway around the world, will glide down to the stratosphere, then to the lower atmosphere, and then land using its jet engines.

A plane that uses sunlight as a source of power has already been flown. Its very large wings are covered with solar cells — devices that change sunlight into electricity. The electricity runs an electric motor, which turns a propeller. So far this plane can carry only a pilot. Someday it may be useful to fly very large-winged planes with solar cells high in the atmosphere of the tropics, where the sun is very strong.

The largest number of aircraft that fly

What is "general aviation"? in the United States and Canada belong to the group called "general aviation." These are small planes that range in size from those that carry only a pilot on short flights, to small jets that carry about a dozen passengers for hundreds of miles. Among them are the planes that land on Arctic ice and on small forest and jungle airstrips. General aviation planes log more miles and carry more passengers than all the scheduled commercial airliners.

RECENT AVIATION HISTORY

Between January 16 and 18, 1957, three U. S. Air Force B-52's, led by Major General Archie J. Old, Jr., flew nonstop around the world. They were refueled in flight by tanker airplanes which met them at several points on their route. The 24,325-mile flight took 45 hours and 19 minutes. The longest flight on a single fueling was made by Major Sidney J. Kubesch, who flew a B-52 from Tokyo over the Arctic to London, an 8,028-mile trip which took 8 hours and 35 minutes. The longest distance in a straight line, 12,532 miles, was flown by Major Clyde R. Evely, in a USAF B-52, from Kadena, Okinawa, to Madrid, Spain, on January 10 and 11, 1962.

* * *

Captain Joseph W. Kittinger, Jr., a thirty-one-year-old United States Air Force officer, soared nearly 103,000 feet above the New Mexico desert in an open-gondola balloon on August 16, 1960. He exceeded the old record set by Lieutenant Colonel David G. Simons, using a closed-gondola balloon, by some 500 feet.

After reaching the record height, Kittinger plunged toward the earth. He set a new world's record for free fall (jumping with a parachute closed). He plunged some 17 miles in 4 minutes and 38 seconds. Upon reaching about 17,500 feet, he opened his parachute and descended the remainder of his trip in 8 minutes and 30 seconds.

A new height-record for a balloon was set May 4, 1961 by Navy Commanders Malcolm Ross and Victor Prather. Their helium-filled balloon, with an aluminum-framed gondola, soared to 113,739 feet. Prather was killed during the helicopter rescue.

On March 5, 1962, Captain Robert G. Sowers flew a Convair B-58 *Hustler* from Los Angeles to New York in 2 hours and 59 minutes. Then, without stopping, he flew back to Los Angeles, making the round trip in 4 hours, 41 minutes, 15 seconds.

* * *

A world record for altitude in horizontal flight was set on May 1, 1965, by Air Force Colonel R. L. Stephens, who flew a Lockheed YF-12A at 80,257.86 feet.

* * *

The longest helicopter flight was made in a Hughes YOH6A, from Culver City, California, to Daytona, Florida, on April 6-7, 1966.

* * *

During the summer of 1966, an X-15 rocket aircraft soared to a height of 324,200 feet, more than 61 miles above the earth, setting a manned winged-craft record. On October 3, 1967, an X-15 flown by Major William J. Knight, USAF, attained a speed of 4,534 miles per hour at Edwards Air Force Base, California.

•

Since the days of Daedalus, man has sought to fly with "his own wings." So far the nearest man has come to that dream has been the *Gossamar Condor*. This plane had cloth-covered wings and a fuselage of very light wood. Its propeller was spun in the same way a bicycle wheel is turned—by a chain attached to pedals. The plane was designed by Paul MacCready and pedaled by Brian Allen, in 1977. Two years later Allen pedaled the *Gossamar Albatross* 22½ miles across the English Channel.

KITTINGER BALLOON

BELL X-15

McDONNELL F4H-1

BOEING 707

DOUGLAS DC-8

GYRODYNE ROTORCYCLE

Rockets, Missiles and Satellites

How were rockets first used? Some historians believe that the Chinese used rockets, similar to our large firecrackers, at about the same time that the ancient Egyptians were building the Great Pyramids. They attached the rockets to arrows to make them fly farther. We do know that in A.D. 1232, during the Mongolian siege of the city of Kaifêng, the Chinese used *fei-i-ho-chien* (sticks of flying fire) to defend themselves. In fourteenth-century Europe, military rockets were used to set fire to cities and terrorize the enemy.

One of the most famous early uses of military rockets was at the Battle of Fort McHenry during the War of 1812. The British launched rockets from boats in conjunction with artillery fire. During the rocket attack, Francis Scott Key, writing the words to the "Star-Spangled Banner," described the red glare of the rockets. Some forty years later, military rockets began to disappear as weapons, because artillery cannons became more efficient.

The first man to attempt to fly a rocket ship was a Chinese mandarin, Wanhu. About A.D. 1500, he had a bamboo chair "rocket ship" to which forty-seven of the largest rockets available were attached. He sat in the chair and held a large kite in each hand. The kites were to help him glide gently back to earth. At a signal, his assistants ignited the rockets. It is reported that there was a great roar, a blast of flame and smoke — and Wanhu and his ship disappeared. There is no doubt that he did not fly into space.

Who were the rocket pioneers? Although rockets disappeared as military weapons shortly after the Mexican War in 1847, they continued to be used for signaling at sea during distress, as flares to light battlefields and as fireworks. But the dream of space continued.

An American physicist, Dr. Robert Goddard, began to experiment with rockets in 1908. In 1919, when he published his first report, he revolutionized rocket theory. Up to that time, scientists believed that a rocket flew because its hot gases shooting out the back pushed against air. Dr. Goddard knew that a rocket flies because of Newton's Third

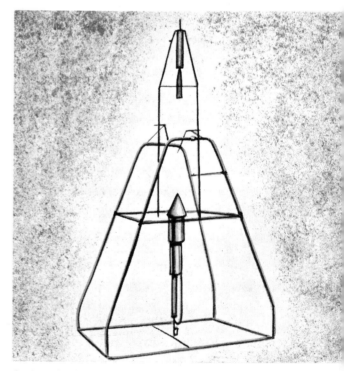

Goddard's first liquid fuel rocket was fired in 1926.

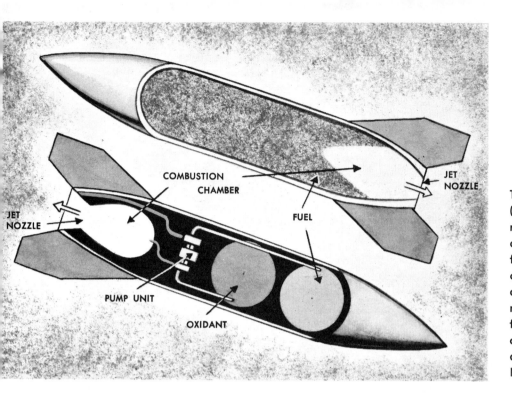

COMBUSTION CHAMBER

JET NOZZLE

JET NOZZLE

FUEL

PUMP UNIT

OXIDANT

The solid fuel rocket (top) is used for short-range guided missiles and as assisting devices for quick take-off of conventional and jet aircraft. The liquid fuel rocket (below) is used for long-range flights and when high speeds are needed, as in launching satellites.

Law of Motion, about which we learned — the same law that causes jet engines to move.

Although people ridiculed him and his work, Dr. Goddard continued to experiment. In 1926, he tested the first liquid fuel rocket. It traveled at 60 miles per hour and reached 184 feet in the air. His report and work inspired others in the field of rocketry. In 1929, in Germany, a rocket-propelled glider carried a man in flight.

In 1935, Dr. Goddard launched a gyroscope-controlled rocket. It rose almost 8,000 feet and attained a speed of almost 700 miles per hour. About the same time, a group of Germans interested in rockets formed the *Verein für Raumschiffahrt,* the Rocket Society. One of its members was Dr. Wernher von Braun who, during World War II, directed rocket research at the German Research Facility at Peenemünde. After the war, von Braun came to the United States where he played a major role in its rocket and space programs.

What makes a rocket fly? The basic rocket engine contains a combustion chamber and an exhaust nozzle. It needs no moving parts. The burning of the propellant (explosive charge or fuel) escaping from the exhaust creates the forward thrust.

Rockets are classified into two general groups — solid propellant and liquid propellant. The first group, solid propellants, are somewhat like the large firecrackers used on the Fourth of July. These rockets are powered by a rapidly burning powder or solid.

Liquid propellant rockets have more complex power units. It is necessary to have tanks within the rockets to hold the liquid and pumps and valves to control the flow of the liquid to the combustion chamber. The *Saturn 1B* and *Saturn 5* launch rockets were the workhorses of the U.S. space program in the 1960's and early 1970's. They used liquid hydrogen for fuel. It was mixed with liquid oxygen (LOX) and was ignited at blast-off.

Because the rockets carry their own oxygen to aid combustion, they can work in outer space where there is no air. Only the amount of fuel limits the height they can reach.

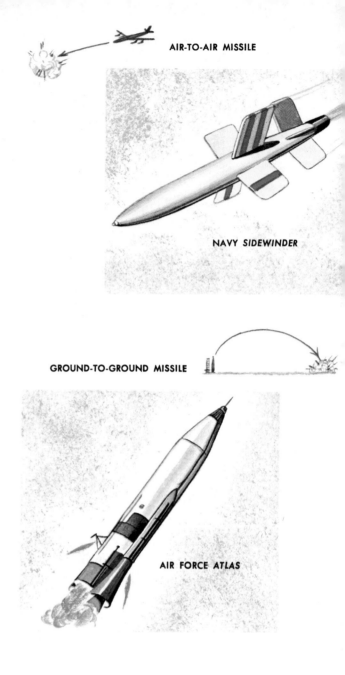

AIR-TO-AIR MISSILE

NAVY *SIDEWINDER*

GROUND-TO-GROUND MISSILE

AIR FORCE *ATLAS*

What is a guided missile? Any rocket whose flight path can be altered in flight is known as a *guided missile*. The Germans' V-1 rockets used during World War II were actually pulsejet engines with explosive warheads to bombard London. These missiles flew at 360 miles per hour and had a range of about 150 miles. The German V-2 rockets were larger and more powerful. Their range was about 200 miles and they reached speeds of 3,600 miles per hour. Once launched, they followed a predetermined ballistic trajectory.

One system of classifying guided missiles is based on (a) where they are fired, and (b) the location of their target. For example, *surface-to-surface* missiles are fired from the ground to hit a target on the ground. Examples of surface-to-surface missiles are the Air Force *Titan* and *Minuteman*. Both have a range of 8,000 to 8,500 miles and travel at a speed of over Mach 20 — twenty times the speed of sound. The Navy's *Poseidon* can be fired from a submarine while it is underwater.

Surface-to-air missiles include the Navy's *Talos* and the Army's *Hercules*, which travel at speeds of over Mach 3 and Mach 4. The Navy's *Sidewinder*, which exceeds a speed of Mach 2.5, is an *air-to-air* missile that is fired from beneath the wings of a fighter plane.

How do they guide missiles? Many guided missiles are controlled in flight by radio, radar, and electronic computers. When one radar beam picks up the target, it feeds the information about height, direction and speed to a computer. The electronic computer makes all the cal-

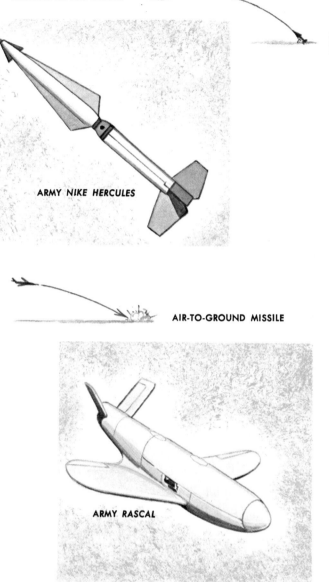

ARMY NIKE HERCULES

AIR-TO-GROUND MISSILE

ARMY RASCAL

culations within seconds and fires the missile. The missile is "watched" in flight by another radar beam, which tells the computer the missile's flight. The computer makes changes in the missile's path by using radio waves which control adjustment motors within the missile.

A similar radar, radio and electronic computer system is used to launch and guide rockets as they go off into space. Large radar and radio telescope units "follow" the rocket as it plunges into space. If the rocket veers off course, these watchers inform the computer and it radios the rocket, making the necessary changes to correct its course.

If you throw a ball into the air, the pull of gravity will bring **Why does a satellite stay up in the sky?** it back to earth. Also, a moving body will continue to travel in a straight line unless acted on by another force. These two principles govern the orbiting of satellites.

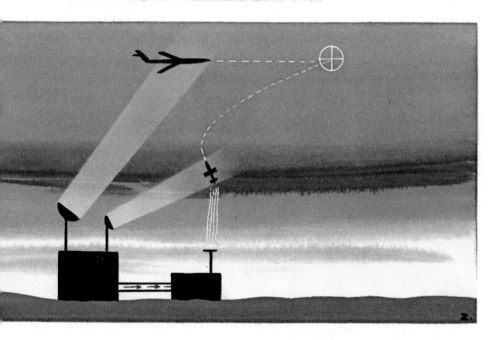

The main radar scanner (left) picks up approaching aircraft. A computer works out the plane's speed, path, height, weather conditions and other factors. The ground missile is automatically made ready and fired by the computer. A smaller radar guides the missile through the air until it reaches the enemy target.

If the ball were shot up like a rocket, it would be affected by these two forces. One is the force of gravity that would pull it back to earth, and the other is the force that would tend to keep it moving in a straight line. Suppose the ball traveled at a speed of 18,000 miles per hour at a height of 300 miles. At this speed and at this height, these two forces would be about equal, or balanced. As a result, the ball would continue to "orbit" the earth. That is what a satellite does.

The speed needed to completely overcome the earth's gravitational pull is called the *escape velocity*. This is the velocity that the body needs to attain to overcome the pull of gravity. That escape velocity from the earth is about 25,000 miles per hour. Thus, for a satellite to remain in orbit, it must attain a speed of at least 18,000 miles per hour. If it is to escape the earth's gravi-

tational pull in order to go into outer space, it must be traveling at over 25,000 miles per hour.

Why do we launch satellites? Man's first artificial satellite was *Sputnik 1,* launched October 4, 1957 by the Soviet Union. The event made large headlines in newspapers and periodicals all over the world. Since then, so many man-made satellites have been sent into space that computers are used to identify each one and keep count. Such launchings have become so commonplace today that most people hardly take note of them.

The United States' first satellite was *Explorer I*, launched February 1, 1958. It discovered that the earth is surrounded by two belts of electrically charged atomic particles.

Now satellites receive from and send to earth radio and television broadcasts. Others have radar that maps the earth's surface and observes conditions in the earth's atmosphere. You have seen TV news broadcasts that show weather maps with clouds over parts of North America. Those maps are made from radar broadcasts sent by satellite.

If a satellite is put into a circular

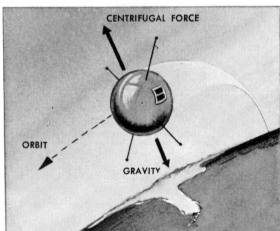

Rockets carry satellite into the air so it can take off under its own power. The satellite is kept in orbit as the centrifugal force is balanced by the gravitational pull of the earth.

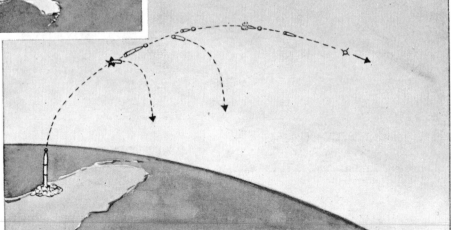

orbit 22,300 miles out in space, it travels exactly as fast as the earth turns on its axis. So the satellite seems to hang stationary in the sky. Also, at 22,300 miles a satellite can broadcast to one-third of the earth's surface. Thus, three such satellites can receive from or broadcast to the whole surface of the earth. Long-distance telephone companies, television and radio broadcasting companies, and military broadcasters all use stationary satellites to broadcast and receive pictures to and from any place on earth.

Artificial satellites carry telescopes to outer space where "seeing" is clearer. Others serve as navigation aids for ships and planes. "Spy satellites" keep watch on military activities. Weather satellites make it possible for forecasters to give warning of approaching storms such as hurricanes.

Stepping-stones Into Space

On October 14, 1947, six miles up in the sky over California, a four-engine B-29 airplane was flying its prescribed course. Fastened to its underside was a smaller plane, painted bright orange. Suddenly, the orange plane, powered by a rocket engine using liquid oxygen and alcohol as fuel, soared upward like a stone fired from a slingshot. That plane was the Bell X-1, a rocket ship piloted by U.S. Air Force Captain Charles E. Yeager. Space and aviation history was made that day as the craft exceeded Mach 1, the speed of sound.

When did man first fly faster than sound?

Six years later, Lt. Colonel Marion Carl flew a Douglas *Skyrocket* to an altitude of 83,235 feet (in August), and made the first flight at *twice* the speed of sound in the same supersonic aircraft (in November).

Other rocket ships included the X-3, the *Flying Stiletto,* and the X-5, the *Flying Guppy.*

In 1963, the X-15, an outstanding rocket ship, was flown to an unofficial height of 354,200 feet by test pilot Joseph A. Walker.

The first step a human being took into space was made by the Soviet Union, on April 12, 1961. Cosmonaut Yuri Gagarin was launched into space in *Vostok I,* a space capsule. He orbited the earth once, reentered the atmosphere, and landed. This feat began a race between the United States and the Soviet Union to explore space with both manned and unmanned spacecraft.

What was man's first step into space?

The United States embarked on a program in three parts. First was *Project Mercury,* in which the National Aeronautics and Space Administration was to learn how to launch and bring back small one-man space capsules. Second was *Project Gemini,* which sent into orbit around the earth two-man spacecraft that could be maneuvered in space. Third was *Project Apollo*, which had the goal of landing a man on the moon.

Although the Soviet Union did not announce its space programs, it concentrated on sending unmanned spacecraft to the moon and the planet Venus. The U.S.S.R. also has launched many large spacecraft that orbited the earth for long periods. In them cosmonauts live and carry out scientific experiments. These spacecraft are called *Salyuts*. The cosmonauts go to them and return in a small craft called a *Soyuz*.

The *Apollo 8, 9*, and *10* spacecraft went

Who landed first on the moon?

to the moon, orbited it, and returned to earth. Then, on July 16, 1969, astronauts Neil A. Armstrong, Edwin E. Aldrin, Jr. and Michael Collins parked *Apollo 11* in orbit around the moon. Armstrong and Aldrin entered a moon-lander vehicle, which separated from the *Apollo* command vehicle and landed on the moon. The first humans on the moon left a memorial plaque saying that they had come in peace for all mankind. They then rocketed up to the orbiting command vehicle, docked with it, and returned to earth.

In the early 1980's the U.S. began a series of flights in *space shuttles*. These had wings like airplanes. They were sent into orbit attached to booster rockets, which then dropped off. When their mission was finished, the shuttles reentered the atmosphere and glided to a landing like an airplane. The first shuttle, *Columbia*, made a successful flight April 12, 1981.

The United States has sent spacecraft to explore other planets. In 1975, *Viking I* and *Viking II* landed on Mars looking for signs of life. Television pictures were sent back. Samples of Martian soil were analyzed and the results were broadcast back to earth.

The United States has sent spacecraft outward in the solar system. They have passed Jupiter, Saturn, and Uranus and have sent back detailed pictures and other information about those giant planets. The most surprising discoveries were that Jupiter, Saturn, and Uranus have many more moons than earthbound astronomers had been able to see. Also, Uranus has faint rings of the kind Saturn has.

The beginning of manned space explo-

What is the price we pay?

ration has not been without a tragic cost in lives of astronauts and cosmonauts. In 1967 three American astronauts died when fire broke out in their sealed space capsule, which was atop an *Apollo* rocket ready to blast into space. The Soviet Union has lost at least four cosmonauts to spacecraft accidents. The worst loss took place on January 28, 1986, when a seal failed on one of the booster rockets launching the space shuttle *Challenger*. The main fuel tank exploded and the shuttle and its crew of seven astronauts were hurled into the Atlantic Ocean. All were killed.

THE HOW AND WHY WONDER BOOK OF
The HUMAN BODY

Written by MARTIN KEEN
Illustrated by DARRELL SWEET
Editorial Production: DONALD D. WOLF

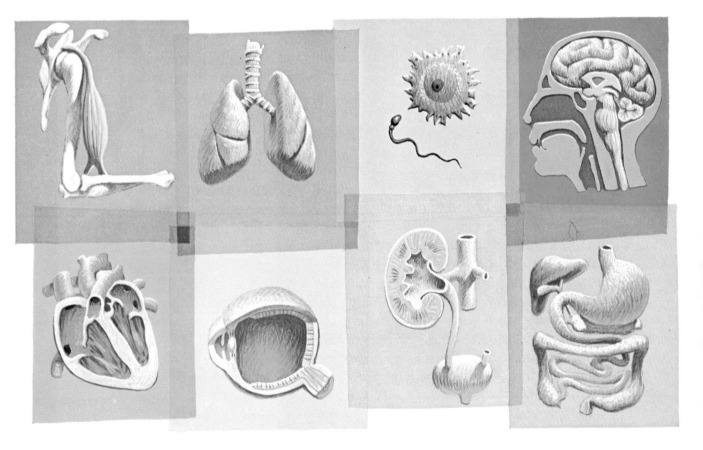

Edited under the supervision of
   Dr. Paul E. Blackwood
   Washington, D. C.

Text and illustrations approved by
   Oakes A. White, Brooklyn Children's Museum, Brooklyn, New York

J.G. Ferguson Publishing Company
Chicago

Introduction

It is the habit of scientists to explore, describe and explain all things in the universe. Little wonder, then, that the human body has been a constant object of study, for it is not only important but very close to home! *The How and Why Wonder Book of the Human Body* tells in a systematic way the most important things scientists and physicians have learned about the subject.

If you simply listened with a stethoscope to the beating of the heart, you might think it was an automatic machine. But if you could tune in on the remarkable activities of the brain cells, you would know that the human body is more than a machine. And as you learn how all the systems work together, you become amazed at what a marvelous organism the human body is. This makes the study of it an exciting adventure, and even though much has been known for centuries about the body, and though more is being discovered every year, there are still many unanswered questions.

The health and well-being of each of us depends on how well we understand our own bodies. This book is written to help us gain that understanding and may encourage many persons to choose a career of service in maintaining the health of others, perhaps as a nurse or doctor. Parents and schools will want to add *The How and Why Wonder Book of the Human Body* to their children's growing shelf of other publications in this series.

Paul E. Blackwood

Dr. Blackwood is a professional employee in the U. S. Office of Education. This book was edited by him in his private capacity and no official support or endorsement by the Office of Education is intended or should be inferred.

Library of Congress Catalog Card Number: 61-16034

ISBN: 0-89434-076-X (set)

Science Library © 1987 J.G. Ferguson Publishing Company
Chicago

CONTENTS

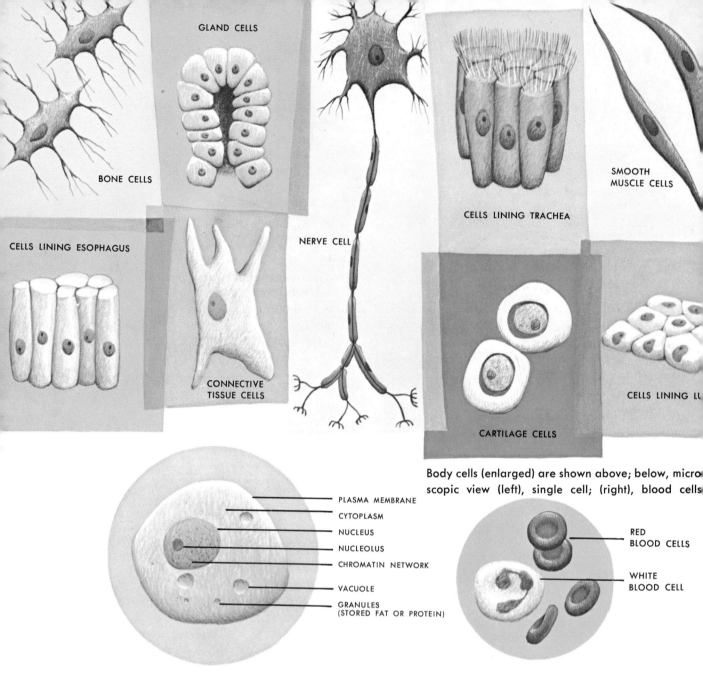

GLAND CELLS

BONE CELLS

CELLS LINING ESOPHAGUS

NERVE CELL

CELLS LINING TRACHEA

SMOOTH MUSCLE CELLS

CONNECTIVE TISSUE CELLS

CARTILAGE CELLS

CELLS LINING L[...]

Body cells (enlarged) are shown above; below, micro scopic view (left), single cell; (right), blood cells

PLASMA MEMBRANE
CYTOPLASM
NUCLEUS
NUCLEOLUS
CHROMATIN NETWORK
VACUOLE
GRANULES (STORED FAT OR PROTEIN)

RED BLOOD CELLS

WHITE BLOOD CELL

The Cell, the Body's Building Material

What do all living things have in common?

Perhaps at some time you have visited a zoo. There you saw huge elephants, tall giraffes, comical little monkeys, strange birds and many other kinds of animals. The animals in the different cages were so different that you must surely believe that they can have little in common.

Yet, all living things actually do have something in common. All living things are made of tiny units, called *cells*. The huge elephant is made of hundreds of billions of cells, and there are little animals whose whole body is but a single cell. The human body, too, is made of cells — billions of them.

Most cells are so small that you need a powerful magnifying lens to see one. Some cells are so small that you could put 250 thousand of them on the period at the end of this sentence. Others, however, are large enough to be seen with the unaided eye. Among these large cells are the root-hairs of plants, certain seaweeds, and the eggs of animals.

What do cells look like?

Cells are of many shapes. Some are round. Others look like bricks with rounded corners. Still others are long and hairlike. Some cells are shaped like plates, cylinders, ribbons or spiral rods.

Looking through a microscope at a single cell from a human body, you can see that the cell is surrounded by membrane. This is the *cell membrane*. It surrounds the cell in the same way that a balloon surrounds the air within itself.

What are the parts of a cell?

Within the cell membrane is a material that has a grainy appearance. This material is *cytoplasm,* which flows about within the cell membrane. Cytoplasm distributes nourishment within the cell and gets rid of the cell's waste products.

Within the cytoplasm is a large dot. This dot is really a sphere and is the cell's *nucleus.* The nucleus is the most important part of the cell. It directs

Tiny units are cells; a group of cells is a tissue; tissues form an organ; organs become unified system.

the cell's living activities. The way in which the cell uses nourishment and oxygen, the way the cytoplasm gets rid of wastes, the way the cell reproduces — all these functions are regulated by the nucleus. If the nucleus is removed, the cell dies.

The cell membrane, the cytoplasm, and the nucleus of all cells are made of a material called *protoplasm.* Protoplasm is a living material and makes a living cell "alive." Scientists have analyzed protoplasm into the elements of which it is made. They have found protoplasm to

Of what material are cells made?

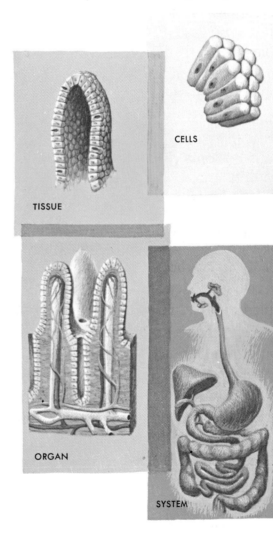

CELLS

TISSUE

ORGAN

SYSTEM

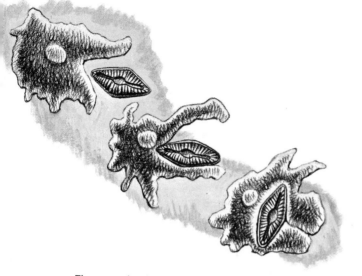

The amoeba is a microscopic mass of protoplasm. It is shown surrounding an organism on which it feeds.

be made of water and many other chemical substances. Although scientists know what these substances are and how much of each there is in protoplasm, no scientist thus far has been able to put them together properly so as to make living protoplasm. This fact tells us that protoplasm is a very complex material.

Cells not only differ in shape, but also **How are cells organized in a human body?** in the work each kind of cell performs within a body. A group of cells, all of the same kind, that performs a particular kind of work, is called a *tissue*. For example, groups of cells that transmit impulses back and forth from the brain to other parts of the body make up nerve tissue. Other kinds of tissue are muscle tissue, connecting tissue, supporting tissue, and epithelial tissue. Epithelial tissue forms the outer layer of the skin, and the surface layer of the cavities in the body, such as the nose, throat, gullet and the stomach.

When different kinds of tissue are organized to perform a particular kind of work within a body, the tissues form an *organ*. An eye is an organ that performs the function of seeing. There are many parts to an eye and each part is made of a particular kind of tissue. When all the tissues of the eye work together while each tissue performs its separate task, then the eye can perform its function of seeing. Other examples of organs are the heart, liver, tongue and lungs.

Organs of the body are organized into unified *systems*. Each system performs a particular task for the body. For example, the digestive system, which includes the mouth, teeth, tongue, gullet, stomach, intestines and many glands, performs the function of digesting food.

Perhaps you have heard an automobile **How is the body like a machine?** repairman say that a car's ignition system needed fixing. Or maybe it was the cooling system or the brake system. Each one of these systems is made up of several parts, and each system performs a particular task in running the car. All systems must work together if the car is to operate. Do you see the similarity between the automobile's systems and the organ systems of a human body?

The human body is a very wonderful machine. It is more complex, better made and can do more kinds of work under more conditions than any machine that man has so far constructed throughout his history.

Man has built giant electronic calculators that can solve mathematical problems in a fraction of the time that a human brain can. Calculating, however, is the only work the giant machine can do. It cannot decide what problems it should work on, nor when it should work on them, as the slower but more versatile human brain can. The great calculating machine, with its limited capacity, takes up all the space around the walls of a large room, but the human brain, with its unlimited capacity, can easily fit into a shoe box.

Why is the body more useful than a machine?

The calculating machine has thousands of parts, but the number of its parts does not even begin to equal the hundreds of millions of unit cells of which the human body is constructed. If the calculating machine breaks down, it must wait for a repairman to fix it. A break or a cut in some part of the human body can usually be repaired by the body itself.

Let us see in detail how this wonderful machine, the human body, works.

The Skin

When you look at a human body, the first thing you see is the *skin*. The average adult human body is covered with about eighteen square feet of skin. The skin varies in thickness. It is very thin over the eyelids, and quite thick on the palms of the hands and the soles of the feet.

How much skin is on a human body?

The skin is composed of two layers. The upper layer is the *epidermis*. This layer is made of dead, flattened cells, which are continually wearing off as we move around.

What are the parts of the skin?

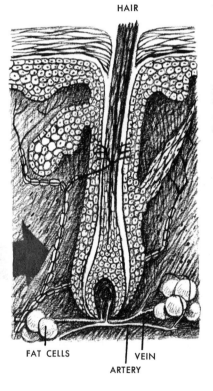

This is a cutaway view of a single hair (right) showing the follicle, which is the opening, or depression, from which the hair grows.

A cross section of human skin (left), shows the epidermis (top layer) and the dermis. The skin represents one of the largest organs of the entire human body.

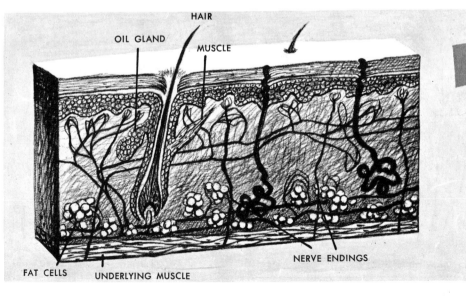

The bottom of the epidermis is made of live cells that die and replace those that wear off on the surface.

Beneath the epidermis is the *dermis*. This layer of skin is made entirely of living cells. There are many small blood vessels and nerve endings in the dermis. Small coiled tubes in this layer open into the epidermis. These tubes are *sweat glands* and their openings are called *pores*. Hairs grow out of the skin and have their roots in the dermis. The openings from which hairs grow are called *hair follicles*.

The skin provides the body with a cov-

What does the skin do? ering that is airtight, waterproof and, when unbroken, a bar to harmful bacteria.

The pigment, or coloring matter, of the skin screens out certain harmful rays of the sun.

The skin helps to regulate the temperature of the body. When the body surface is cold, the blood vessels in the skin contract and force blood deeper into the body. This prevents the body from losing much heat by radiation. When the body is too warm, the same blood vessels expand and bring more blood to the surface of the skin. This allows the body to lose heat by radiation. Also, the sweat glands pour out perspiration. The perspiration evaporates, and since evaporation is a cooling process, the skin is further cooled.

When perspiration flows out of the

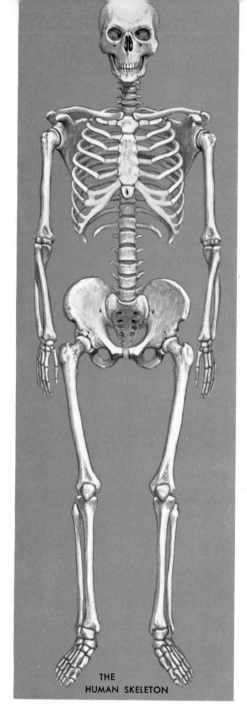

THE
HUMAN SKELETON

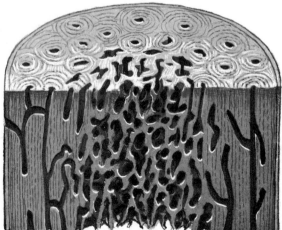

Cross section of human bone. Adults have 206 bones.

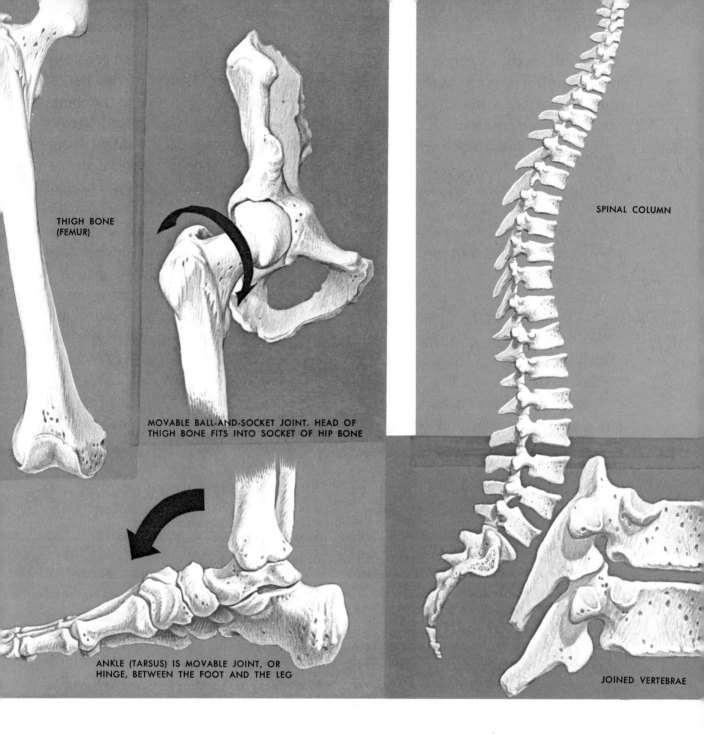

THIGH BONE
(FEMUR)

MOVABLE BALL-AND-SOCKET JOINT. HEAD OF
THIGH BONE FITS INTO SOCKET OF HIP BONE

SPINAL COLUMN

ANKLE (TARSUS) IS MOVABLE JOINT, OR
HINGE, BETWEEN THE FOOT AND THE LEG

JOINED VERTEBRAE

pores, it carries with it certain dissolved body wastes.

The skin is a sense organ because there are many nerve endings in the skin.

Although people do not ordinarily consider the skin to be an organ of the body, you can see by its structure and all the things it performs for the body that it really is an organ.

The Bones

If you suddenly removed the poles from a circus tent, the

What is the purpose of the skeleton?

tent would collapse. The poles support the soft, pliable canvas of the tent. They also help to give the tent its shape. The *bones* of the human skeleton support the softer parts of the body

9

and give the body its general shape. If the skeleton of a body were suddenly removed, the body would sink to the floor in a shapeless mass.

The bones also help to protect the softer parts of the body. The skull forms a strong case for the very soft brain. Two bony sockets in front of the skull protect the eyes. The spinal column forms a bony tube that protects the delicate spinal cord. The ribs form a hard elastic framework that protects the heart and lungs. If a person had no ribs and bumped into someone, even a small bump might collapse the lungs or damage the heart.

Bones also provide anchors to which muscles are attached, and bones provide leverage for the movement of the muscles.

There are two other things that bones do for the body: the inner parts of some bones make blood cells; and bones are the body's chief storage place for calcium, a chemical element very important to the sound health of the body.

What is the structure of a bone? You can see, by looking at a cutaway view of a bone, that it consists of two main kinds of material: a dense outer material and a spongy, porous inner material. The hard outer material, that gives a bone its shape and strength, is made mostly of compounds of the chemical elements *calcium* and *phosphorus*. The soft inner part of the bone is called *marrow*. Most marrow is yellowish in color. It is made up of fat cells and is simply a storage depot for fat. Toward the ends of long bones, like those of the arms and legs, and generally throughout the interior of flat bones, such as those of the skull and the spinal column, there are patches and streaks of reddish tissue. This reddish tissue gets its color from red blood cells.

Long bones are generally cylindrical in shape. The long, cylindrical portion of these bones is called the *shaft*. The ends of the long bones are thicker than the shaft, and are shaped so that they may fit into the ends of adjoining bones. The short bones, such as those of the wrist and ankle, are composed mostly of a thick shaft of elastic, spongy material inside a thin covering of hard bone material. Flat bones, such as the ribs, are made up of spongy material between two plates of hard bone.

How many bones are there in the human body? An infant may have as many as 350 bones, but as the child grows older, many of these bones grow together to form single bones. A normal adult has 206 bones. Some adults may have a bone or two more, because the bones they had as infants did not grow together correctly. Some adults have a bone or two less, because the growing-together process went too far, and two bones of their ankles or wrists that should have remained separate may have grown together.

The skull is made up of twenty-nine bones. The round part of the skull, the part that encases the brain, is called the *cranium,* and consists of eight bones. The face, including the lower jaw, consists of fourteen bones. There are three tiny bones in each ear. And

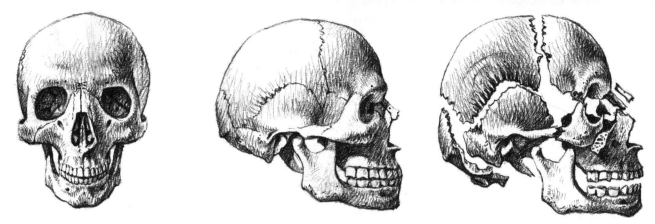

Front view of the human skull (left); side view (center); and side view with bones separated (right). The cranium, the part of the skull enclosing the brain, is composed of bones which are held together by immovable joints.

there is a single bone — the *hyoid bone* — in the throat.

The spinal column consists of twenty-six hollow cylinders of bone called *vertebrae*. If you strung together twenty-six spools of thread on a stiff wire in the shape of a very open letter S, you would have constructed something that looks much like the human spinal column.

The chest consists of twenty-five bones: one breast bone, called the *sternum,* and twenty-four ribs. Seven pairs of ribs attach to the spinal column at one end and the sternum at the other. Three pairs of ribs attach only to the spinal column, curve around to the front, but do not meet the sternum. And two pairs of ribs, called *floating ribs,* extend from the spine only part-way around to the front.

There are two collar bones, and two shoulder bones. Each arm consists of one upper-arm bone and two lower-arm bones. There are eight bones in the wrist. The palm of each hand is made up of five bones, and fourteen bones make up the fingers of a hand.

There are two hip bones. Each leg has one thigh bone, one kneecap, one shinbone, and one bone on the other side of the lower leg.

The ankle of each foot consists of seven bones and the foot, itself, of five, while fourteen bones make up the toes of each foot.

Every bone in the body — except one — meets with another bone. The one bone that does not meet another bone is the U-shaped hyoid bone in the throat.

How are the bones connected?

The meeting places of the bones are called *joints*. There are two kinds of joints: those about which the adjoining bones do not move, and those about which the bones do move freely. The bones of the cranium are held together by joints of the first kind. These are immovable joints.

Holding these bones together is a kind of very tough, springy tissue, called *cartilage*. Cartilage also joins together the bones of the spinal column. The springy nature of cartilage makes it a good shock absorber. If the lower parts of the spine receive a blow, the cartilage rings that join each vertebra to the one above it, absorb the shock, so that the brain does

What holds the bones together?

11

not feel the blow. If this were not so, every time you took a step, your brain would receive a jolt.

The bones at movable joints are held

What are ligaments? together by thick cords of tough, stringy tissue called *ligaments*. To aid movement, at least one of the two adjoining bones has a small hollow that contains a lubricating fluid. This fluid helps the bones move smoothly over one another, just as oil helps the parts of an engine move over one another.

All the bones of the body and their connecting cartilage and ligaments make up the body's *skeletal system*.

The Muscular System

The bones of the human body have no

What are the muscles? way of moving themselves. The muscles of the body move the bones and there are more than 600 muscles to move the parts of the skeleton. Muscles make up more than half the weight of the human body.

Muscles are made of bunches of

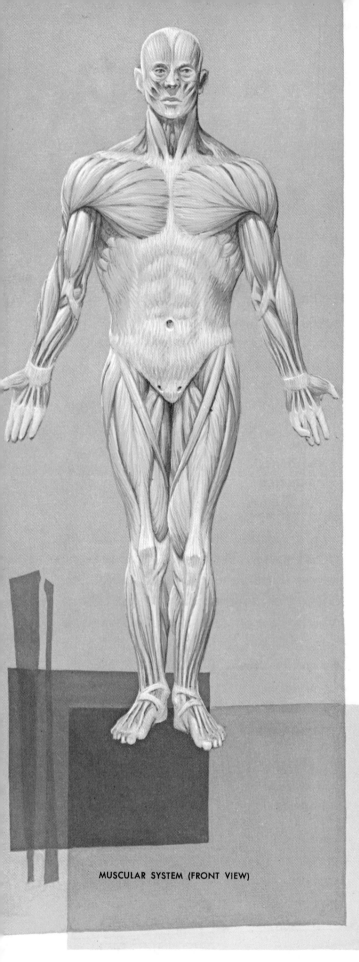

MUSCULAR SYSTEM (FRONT VIEW)

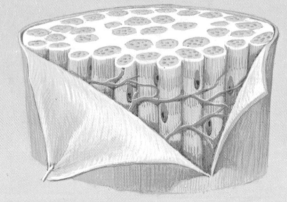

CROSS SECTION THROUGH MUSCLE

muscular tissue held tightly together. Muscular tissue is very fibrous, so that a muscle is somewhat like a bunch of rubber bands bound tightly together.

Beef is the muscle of steers. With a pin,

How can you see muscle fibers?

pick apart a piece of roast beef. You will easily be able to separate it into long, thin strands that are fibers of muscle tissue. If you have a microscope, place a very thin muscle fiber under a cover-glass upon a glass slide. You will then be able to see that muscle tissue is made up of spindle-shaped cells.

A typical muscle is thick in the middle

How are muscles attached to bones?

and tapers gradually toward the ends. It is the ends of a muscle that are attached to bones. One end of a muscle is anchored to a bone that the muscle cannot move. This attachment is called the *origin* of the muscle. The other end is attached to a bone that the muscle is intended to move. This attachment is called the *insertion* of the muscle. For example, the

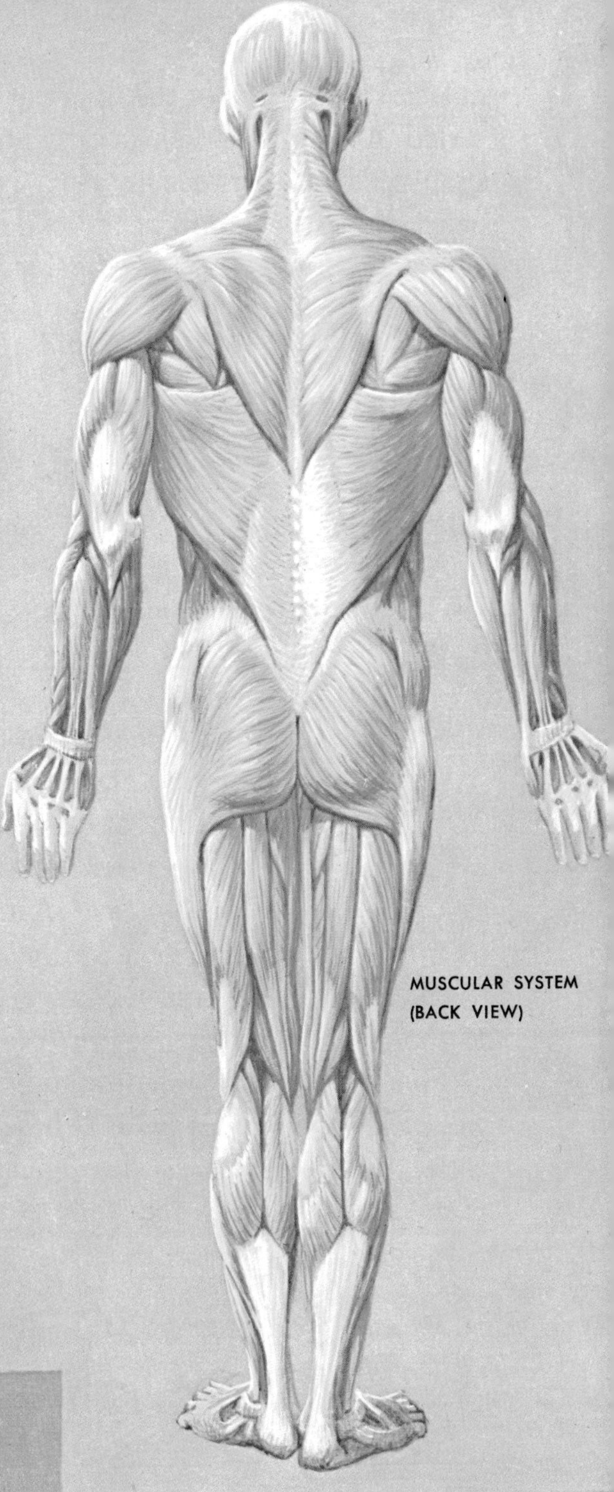

MUSCULAR SYSTEM
(BACK VIEW)

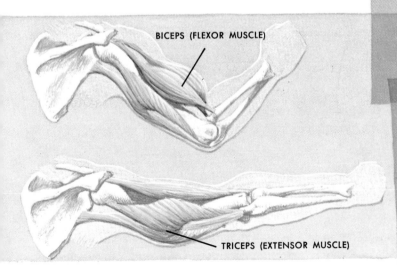

BICEPS (FLEXOR MUSCLE)

TRICEPS (EXTENSOR MUSCLE)

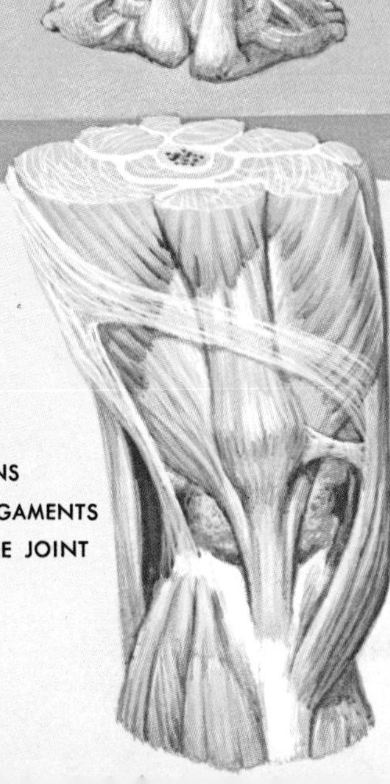

TENDONS
AND LIGAMENTS
OF KNEE JOINT

muscle at the front of the upper arm — called the *biceps* — has its origin at the shoulder bone, and its insertion is just below the elbow joint on the bone that is on the thumb side of the forearm. The actual attachment of the end of a muscle to a bone is usually accomplished by a short, tough cord of much the same kind of tissue that makes up ligaments. This connective cord is called a *tendon*.

All the muscles of the body and their tendons make up the *muscular system* of the body.

The muscles that move the skeleton are

What are the two kinds of muscle?

ones that we can move at will. They are called *voluntary muscles*. Among them are the ones that move the eyes, tongue, soft palate and the upper part of the gullet.

There are muscles in the body that we cannot move at will. These are called *involuntary muscles*. This type of muscle is found in the walls of veins and arteries, stomach, intestines, gall bladder, the lower parts of the gullet and in several other internal organs. Thousands of tiny involuntary muscles in the skin move the hair. When you are chilled or frightened and have goose flesh, or goose pimples, the little lumps on your skin are due to the tiny muscles in the skin pulling your hairs erect.

The eye provides a good distinction be-

What are the differences in muscles?

tween voluntary and involuntary muscles. Voluntary muscles enable you to control the movements of your eye, in order to look in the direction you wish. However, you cannot control at will the muscle that widens and narrows the pupil of your eye. This muscle is involuntary.

But the distinction between voluntary and involuntary muscles does not always hold true. For instance, when you shiver with cold or fright, the muscles that shake your body are voluntary muscles. Ordinarily, you can control these muscles, but , when shivering, you have no control over either starting or stopping the action of these muscles.

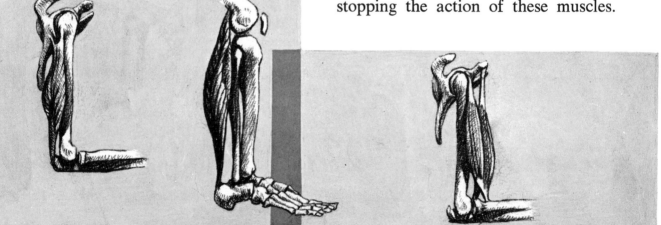

Lowering the arm (left) is an example of a first-class lever, as in a seesaw; rising on the toes (center), a second-class lever, as in a rowing oar; flexing, or "making a muscle" (right), a third-class lever, as in a fishing rod.

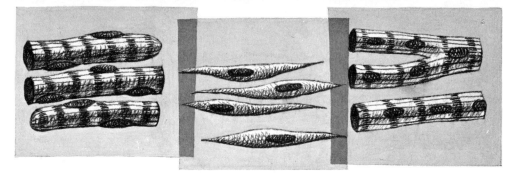

The stringlike matter making up voluntary muscles is known as fiber. Three kinds of muscle fiber are shown here (left to right): skeletal, smooth, cardiac.

They act as if they were involuntary. Certain circus performers can swallow various objects, and then, at will, bring them up without difficulty. These performers have learned to control their involuntary stomach and lower-gullet muscles, as though they were voluntary muscles.

Muscle tissue is made of cells whose cytoplasm can contract. When the muscle contracts, it becomes short, and thereby pulls on the bone in which it is inserted. When you want to show someone how strong you are and you "make a muscle" by contracting your biceps, your forearm is pulled up toward your shoulder. If you want to lower your arm, you relax your biceps and contract your *triceps,* the muscle on the underside of the arm. The contraction of the triceps pulls the forearm straight. You can see that the two muscles of the upper arm work as a team or pair. All the voluntary muscles of the body work in pairs.

How do muscles move?

One way to increase the power used to do work is to apply that power to a lever. A lever is a device that increases work power or range of motion. The joints in the human body act as

How do joints help muscles to move bones?

levers that increase the power of a muscle or increase the distance through which the muscle can move a bone.

If you raise yourself on your toes, you are making use of one kind of lever. The muscles that form the calves of your legs have to do the work of lifting your whole body. You would need to have much larger calf muscles if they had to undergo the strain of lifting your body by a direct pull. Yet you easily raise yourself on your toes, because your foot acts as a lever.

In the act of raising yourself on your toes, your weight bears straight down on the point where your shinbone rests on your ankle bone. The muscles of your calf pull upward on your heel bone, and your foot pivots upward on the fulcrum — the point around which the lever moves — which is formed by the bones that make up the ball of your foot. (Although we say that we raise ourselves on our toes, we actually raise ourselves on the balls of our feet and steady ourselves with our toes.)

If you reach down and grasp the back of your foot just above your heel, you can feel the strong tendon — called the *Achilles tendon*—that connects the muscles of your calf to your heel bone. If, now, you raise yourself on the ball of your foot, you can feel the calf muscles tighten and bulge as they contract and pull upward on your heel.

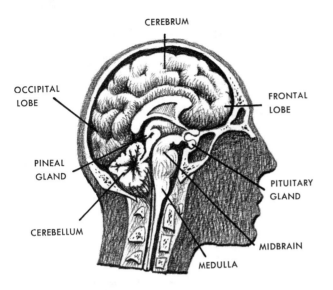

Cutaway view of the skull showing location of brain.

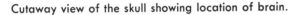

Parts of the brain control several of our activities.

The Brain and Nerves

Suppose you have dropped your pencil on the floor and want to pick it up. This is a very easy thing to do, something you can accomplish with hardly any thought or difficulty. Yet this simple action causes you to use dozens of your voluntary muscles.

What controls the movements of the body?

First, you have to locate the pencil. This requires you to move your eyes, and probably also to turn your head, until you have brought the pencil into view. Then you must bend down to reach the pencil, grasp it, and then straighten up again. Not only do dozens of voluntary muscles bring about your motions, but they must do so in just the right order. It would be futile to attempt to grasp the pencil before you bent down to bring your hand within reach. Clearly something is controlling the motions of your muscles. What is it?

The movements of your muscles are controlled by your brain which works through a system of nerves distributed throughout your body. The brain and the nerves, together, make up the body's *nervous system*.

The brain occupies the upper half of the skull. The largest part of the brain, called the *cerebrum*, consists of two deeply-wrinkled hemispheres of nerve tissue, one hemisphere on each side of the head.

What is the cerebrum?

All of man's conscious activities are controlled by his cerebrum. It enables him to remember, perceive things, solve problems and understand meanings — in short, to think. Thanks to man's most highly-developed cerebrum, he is the most intelligent of all animals.

At the back of the skull, and almost covered by the cerebrum, is the *cerebellum*. This part of the brain, too, consists of two hemispheres.

What is the cerebellum?

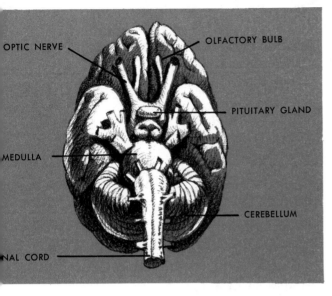

OPTIC NERVE   OLFACTORY BULB

PITUITARY GLAND

MEDULLA

CEREBELLUM

NAL CORD

An undersurface view of the brain showing its parts.

The brain and spinal cord make up the central nervous system. The nerves which branch out of this nervous system form the peripheral nervous system.

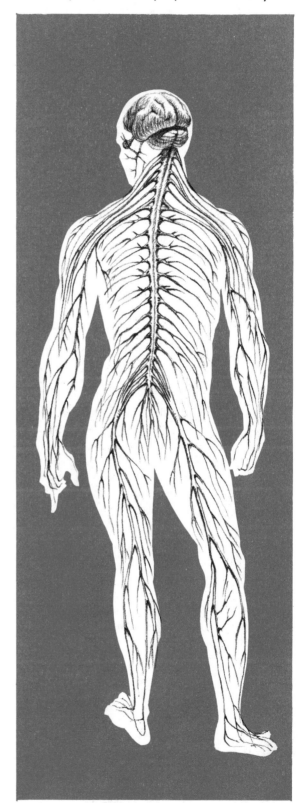

The cerebellum coordinates muscular activity. It is the cerebellum that is responsible for man's ability to learn habits and develop skills. As an infant you learned, after many tries and falls, to stand upright. Learning to walk was another accomplishment that took much time and effort. Now, standing and walking are habits to which you need give no thought, yet both these activities require the use of many muscles in exactly the right order. The cerebellum automatically controls these muscles.

Have you learned to skate or ride a bicycle? At first, you had to think about each move you made, but soon the movements became automatic, so that you did not have to think unless an unusual situation arose. When you were learning, your cerebrum was in control of your movements as you thought about just which muscles you were going to use next. Later, when you knew how to make each movement correctly, your cerebellum took over con-

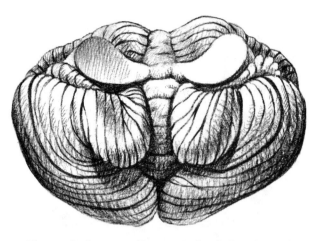

The cerebellum coordinates man's mind and muscles.

trol from your cerebrum. Although the cerebellum's muscular control is automatic, it is important to remember that the muscles it controls are voluntary muscles.

The involuntary muscles are controlled **What is the medulla?** by a small part of the brain that is at the top of the spinal cord. This is the *medulla*. It is a little more than an inch long and is really a thickening

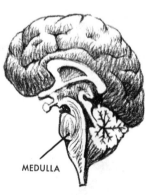

The medulla is a bulblike enlargement of the spinal cord. It carries and sends out nerve impulses which control circulation of blood, breathing, digestion and other processes, too.

MEDULLA

of the spinal cord. The medulla controls the beating of the heart, the rate of breathing, the movements of the stomach and intestines, the movements of the gullet when swallowing and other vital activities of the body.

The *spinal cord* extends downward from **What does the spinal cord look like?** the medulla through the protecting bony rings of the spinal column. The cord is cylindrical in shape, with an outer covering of supporting cells and blood vessels, and an inner, H-shaped core of nerve fibers. The spinal cord extends through four-fifths the length of the spine, and is a little longer in men than in women, averaging sixteen and one-half inches in length. It weighs just about one ounce.

Twelve pairs of nerves branch off the spinal cord and pass through the base of the skull into the brain. Thirty-one other pairs branch off the spinal cord throughout its length. These nerve branches run to all the organs of the body, where they branch again and again, until the smallest branches are nerves which are so thin that they cannot be seen with the unaided eye.

Nerves that extend upward from the spinal cord to the brain pass through the medulla where they cross. Thus, the left side of the brain controls the right side of the body, while the right side of the brain controls the left side of the body.

An army division is composed of many **How is the nervous system like an army telephone network?** thousands of men who perform a wide variety of duties. In order to control the activities of so many soldiers, it is necessary to have some system by which the commanding general can learn what is going on in all the units of his division and thus, to give orders to any of these units. In order to accomplish this, a telephone network is set up.

When a battle is in progress, soldiers posted near the battle line can telephone reports of action back to their headquarters in order to inform the general of the situation. The general gets the messages from these posts. Using this information, and calling on his training and experience, he issues orders to be followed by soldiers under his command. These orders travel back along the same telephone wires.

Let us follow a similar situation within the human body. Let us suppose that you have accidently knocked a pencil off your desk and want to pick it up. When the sound of the falling pencil reaches your ears, it causes elec-

trical impulses to move from your ears along two nerves — auditory nerves — and then to your brain. Your ears are similar to the posts near the battle line, your nerves similar to the telephone wires, and the electrical impulses similar to the messages that move along the wires.

When the brain receives electrical impulses from the ears, a particular part of the cerebrum perceives the impulses as sound, and passes this information on to another part of the cerebrum, one that is concerned with recognition. This part of the brain calls on the part that stores information —

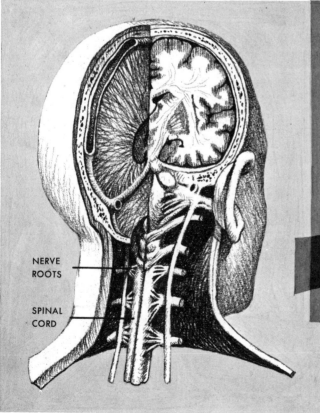

NERVE ROOTS

SPINAL CORD

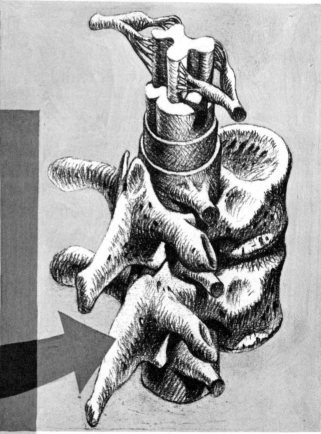

(Left): Cutaway view of back of the head. (Above): Part of the backbone, also known as the spine, spinal column and vertebral column. It consists of bones called vertebrae which surround the spinal cord.

19

the memory. If you have ever before heard a pencil fall, your memory recognizes the sound. Now, you are aware of what has happened.

This situation is similar to that of the general who gets battle reports, and then calls on his training and past experience to help him get a clear picture of what is taking place at the battle-front.

Once your brain is aware of the fallen pencil, it decides to pick up the pencil. Electrical impulses go from your brain to the muscles of your eyes, which then move about seeking to bring the pencil into view. This is similar to that of the general who sends messages to front-line posts asking for more information on the battle.

When the pencil is brought into view, electrical impulses flash back to your cerebrum, which must again go through the processes of perception and recognition, in order to identify the pencil. Here we have new reports coming back to the commanding general who interprets them.

Having located the pencil, your cerebrum now sends hundreds of electrical impulses along nerves to the many muscles that must be moved when you bend over, reach out your arm, close your fingers around the pencil, and then straighten up again. These impulses and the responding muscular movements are similar to messages from the general going out over the telephone wires and the soldiers acting upon the general's orders.

Nerve cells, also called *neurons,* are **What are nerve cells?** specially constructed so as to carry nerve impulses from one part of the body to another. Nerve tissue can conduct extremely small amounts of electricity. Nerve impulses are actually small amounts of electricity.

Each neuron has a central portion, or **What are the parts of a neuron?** *cell body,* that has a nucleus, cytoplasm and a cell membrane. From one side of the cell body there extend very slender branching threads of protoplasm.

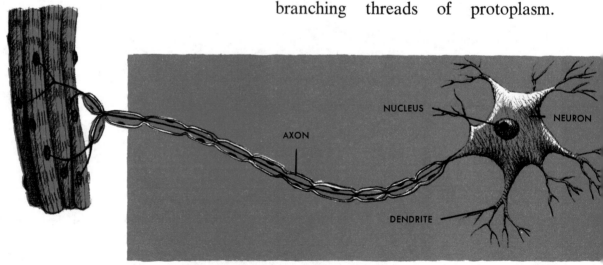

NUCLEUS

AXON

NEURON

DENDRITE

Nerve impulses from a neuron travel to the nerve endings of a muscle (left).

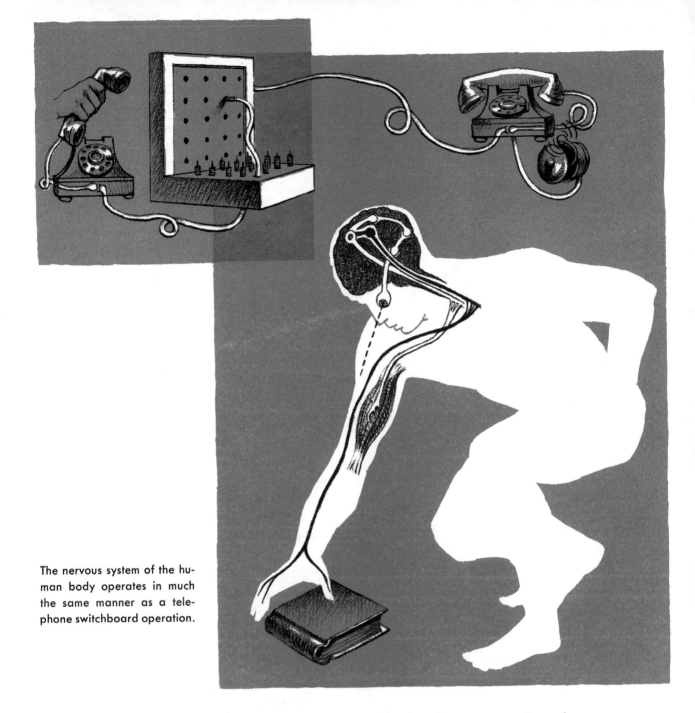

The nervous system of the human body operates in much the same manner as a telephone switchboard operation.

These tiny nerve fibers are called *dendrites*. They look much like twigs at the end of a tree branch. From the other side of the cell body there extends a fairly thick nerve fiber — surrounded by a fatty sheath — which ends in slender, branching threads of protoplasm. These nerve fibers are called *axons*. Some axons are very short, while others are as much as three feet long. Dendrites conduct nerve impulses to the cell body. Axons carry impulses away from the cell body.

Nerve tissue is made up of a series of neurons arranged so that the branching threads of protoplasm of an axon intermingle with the dendrites of the neighboring neuron. However, the two sets of branches do not actually touch. The gap between the branches is called a *synapse*. When an impulse moves along a nerve, it must jump across the syn-

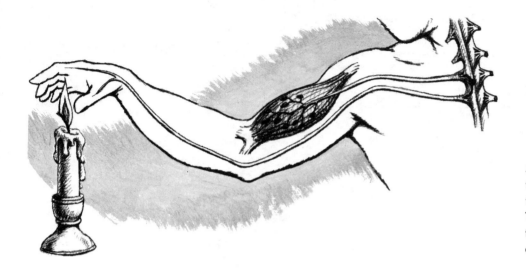

A simple reflex action takes place when you touch a candle flame. The arm muscles contract and you pull your arm away very quickly.

apse between one neuron and its neighbor.

Nerves are divided into two kinds: *sensory nerves* that carry impulses from sense organs to the brain, and *motor nerves* that carry command impulses to the muscles.

If you touch a very hot radiator, you

What is a reflex action?

quickly jerk your hand away. You do not think about pulling your hand away — you act automatically. This automatic action is called a *reflex action*.

In a reflex action, the nerve impulse takes a special pathway, called a *reflex arc*. In the case of your touching the hot radiator, the impulse moved from the skin where it came in contact with the radiator along a sensory nerve to your spinal cord. Here the impulse set off another impulse in a motor nerve running from your spinal cord to your arm muscles. The muscles contracted and pulled your hand away from the radiator. This action took place in about one-tenth of a second.

At the same time, the original sensory impulse traveled up your spinal cord to your brain, where you felt it as pain.

Reflex actions are very useful in pro-

How are reflex actions helpful?

tecting the body from harm. If you had to think about what movements to make

when suddenly threatened with harm, you might become confused and do the wrong thing. The automatic action of your reflexes usually causes you to act correctly and quickly enough to avoid or lessen the danger threatening you. For example, if you suddenly become aware of an object flying through the air toward your face, reflex actions cause you to dodge the object and to close your eyes tightly.

Sit comfortably in a chair, and cross

How can you demonstrate a reflex action?

your right leg over the upper part of your left leg. Feel around just below the

kneecap of your right leg for a tendon

that runs downward from the kneecap. With the edge of the fingers of your right hand strike this tendon sharply — though not too hard, of course. If you do this correctly, the lower part of your right leg will jump upward, bending from the knee joint. After you have learned to cause this reflex action, wait a few minutes and try it again. This time, you may note that your leg is already in motion before you feel your fingers strike the knee.

The Senses

What are the senses? We are made aware of the world around us by means of our *senses*. For many centuries, man believed that human beings had only five senses: *sight, hearing, touch, smell,* and *taste*. Modern scientists have added to the list the senses of *pressure, heat, cold* and *pain*.

There are several steps in the process of sensing. A stimulus acts on the nerves in one of the sense organs. Nerve impulses from the sense organ travel to the brain. In the brain, the impulses are interpreted as a feeling or sensation. For instance, if you stick your finger with a needle, nerve endings in the skin of your finger are stimulated to send impulses to your brain, which interprets the impulses as pain.

It is important to note that, although the brain interprets the impulses as pain, the pain is not felt in the brain, but rather in the finger; that is, the sense organ.

What does the eye look like? The organs of sight are the *eyes*. A human eye is shaped like a ball and is about an inch in diameter. The eye is surrounded by a tough white protective covering. At the front of the eye, there is a transparent circular portion in this covering. Just behind this transparent portion is a space filled with a clear liquid. At the back of this space is a circular tissue with a hole in it. The tissue is called the *iris*, and the hole is the *pupil*. The iris is the colored part of the eye. On the

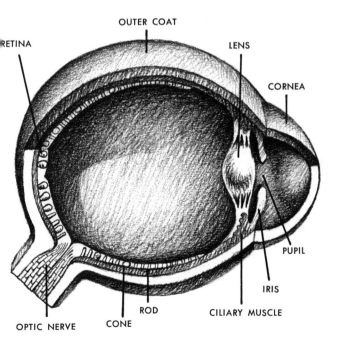

CROSS SECTION OF THE HUMAN EYE

RETINA
OUTER COAT
LENS
CORNEA
PUPIL
IRIS
CILIARY MUSCLE
ROD
CONE
OPTIC NERVE

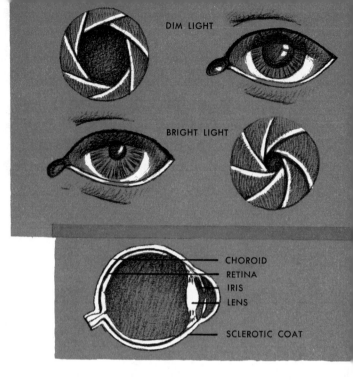

DIM LIGHT

BRIGHT LIGHT

CHOROID
RETINA
IRIS
LENS

SCLEROTIC COAT

inner edge of the iris, around the pupil, is a ring of tiny muscles sensitive to light. In bright light, these muscles contract and narrow the pupil. In dim light, the muscles relax and widen the pupil.

If you stand in front of a mirror in a brightly-lit room, you can easily see the pupil of your eye widen and narrow. Cover one eye with your hand for about a minute and a half. Suddenly remove your hand, and look at the eye that was covered. You will see the pupil narrow.

Behind the iris is a transparent circular lens made of tough tissue. **How do we see?** Muscles attached to the rim of this lens can focus it upon near or far objects. A beam of light passing through the lens is turned upside down and is reversed from right to left. After passing through the lens, light traverses a large spherical cavity that makes up the bulk of the eye. This cavity is filled with a clear liquid through which light passes easily. Around the inner surface of this cavity is a coating of special nerve endings that are sensitive to light. This sensitive coating is the *retina*. The nerve endings connect with the *optic nerve* that leads to the brain.

Light, reflected from an object and entering the eye, is focused by the lens as a reversed image on the retina. The nerve impulses arriving at the brain from the retina are interpreted as an image of the object.

This interpretation also reverses the directions of the image as it was projected on the retina, so that we do not see things upside down and backward.

At the point where the optic nerve enters the eye, there is **What is the blind spot?** no retina, and consequently, this area is not light-sensitive. This point, which is just below the center of the back of the eye, is called the *blind spot*.

You can prove the existence of this blind spot in the following manner. Note the cross and the dot on this page. Close your left eye, and hold this page before your open right eye. Fix your gaze on the cross. Now move the book toward you and then away from you, until you find the point where the dot completely disappears. At this point the dot is focused by the lens of the eye exactly on your blind spot. Hence, you can't see the dot.

✚   ●

Place a table directly beneath a light, so that objects near **Why do we see better with two eyes than with one?** the center of the table cast no shadows. Stand about eight feet in front of the

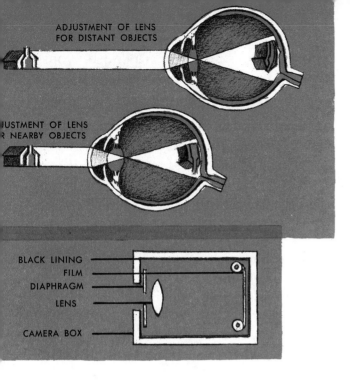

ADJUSTMENT OF LENS
FOR DISTANT OBJECTS

ADJUSTMENT OF LENS
FOR NEARBY OBJECTS

BLACK LINING
FILM
DIAPHRAGM
LENS
CAMERA BOX

The characteristics and operation of both the human eye and the camera eye show remarkable similarity.

table. Crouch down so that your eyes are on a level with the top of the table, and close one eye.

Ask someone to stand a thread-spool at the center of the table. Also ask him to place another spool of the same size about four inches in front or in back of the first spool, but not to tell you whether the second spool is before or behind the first. Try to guess the location of the second spool. Try this several times, keeping a record of your correct guesses. You will probably have a poor score.

With both eyes open, repeat your guessing. This time, you should have a nearly-perfect score. Why?

When we look at an object with both eyes, a slightly different image is projected on the retina of each eye. This is true because each eye sees the object from a slightly different angle. The result is that the brain's interpretation of the two images provides the viewer with a single, three-dimensional image of the object. The two images also pro-

vide the viewer with a perception of depth that enables him to make judgments of farness and nearness. This is why you had a better score when judging the locations of the spools with both eyes open.

The *ears* are the organs of hearing. The

What does the ear look like?

part of the ear on the outside of the head helps to a slight extent to direct sound waves into the ear. Sound waves entering the ear strike the eardrum, or *tympanic membrane,* and cause it to vibrate. This membrane stretches taughtly across the whole diameter of the ear passage. Touching the inner surface of the eardrum is a tiny bone called the *malleus* or hammer. The malleus connects by a joint to another little bone, the *incus* or anvil. And the incus is jointed to a third bone, the *stapes* or stirrup — so named because it looks like a stirrup. Below

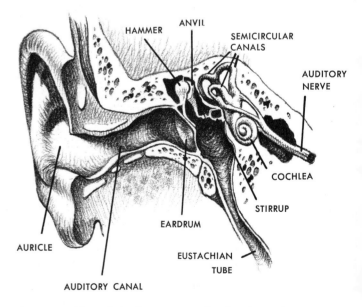

HAMMER ANVIL SEMICIRCULAR CANALS AUDITORY NERVE COCHLEA STIRRUP EARDRUM EUSTACHIAN TUBE AURICLE AUDITORY CANAL

A cross section of the human ear, showing its parts.

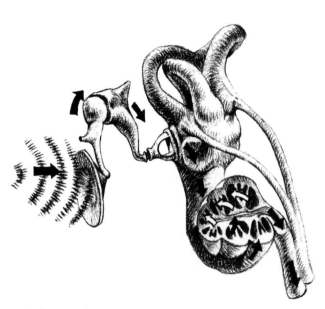

Arrows show path of sound through the inner ear.

and inward from the stirrup are three small cavities filled with liquid that are separated from each other by membranes. The innermost of these membranes connects with nerves that go to the brain.

When sound waves cause the eardrum

How do we hear? to vibrate, the eardrum causes the malleus to vibrate, too. The vibrating malleus strikes against the incus with each vibration. The incus passes the vibration to the stirrup, which, in turn, causes the liquid in the cavities to vibrate. Vibration in the innermost cavity sets up impulses in the nerves that go to the cerebrum. That part of the cerebrum concerned with the sense of hearing interprets the impulses as sound.

This complicated system works remarkably well. It can make you aware of a very wide range and complex combination of sounds, such as those which reach your ear when you are in the presence of an orchestra. Also, your hearing organs can be activated by such small volumes of sound as those which come from a pencil moving over a sheet of paper on the other side of a room from the hearer.

Blindfold yourself with a handkerchief,

Why do we hear better with two ears than with one? and sit on a chair placed in the middle of a room. Ask someone to move quietly to any part of the room and clap his hands once. Point to where you think he is. Repeat this activity several times as your aide moves quietly from place to place about the room. Have your helper keep score of the number of times you have pointed correctly to the location at which he clapped his hands.

Place a hand tightly over one ear, and repeat the whole experiment. Repeat it a third time, covering the other ear.

If your sense of hearing is normal, you will find that your score of correct locations was poorer when you listened with only one ear. From this you can readily understand that using two ears gives you a better perception of sound direction, just as using two eyes gives you a better perception of visual depth.

The organ of smell is the *nose*. When

Why do we smell odors? taking a breath, you may draw into your nose certain gases intermingled with the gases of which air is made. When the added gases come into contact with a small patch of epithelial cells on the upper part of the inner surface of your nose, the cells cause impulses to travel along a pair of nerves to your cerebrum, where the impulses are interpreted as odors.

Just how this process takes place is not clearly known. However, since the inside of the nose is always damp, scientists believe that the odorous gases dissolve in the dampness and cause a chemical reaction that stimulates nerve endings in the epithelial cells. This causes the cells to send impulses along the nerves.

Not all gases react with the organ of smell to set up sensations of odor. This is why we call only certain gases — those that do react — odors or smells. The more of an odorous gas that comes into contact with the organ of smell, the stronger is the sensation of odor. This is why we usually draw deep breaths when we sniff about to locate the source of an odor.

Can the sense of smell get "tired" or "lost"? The sense of smell seems to become fatigued easily; that is, the sensation of odor fades after a short time. Perhaps you have entered a room in which you found a strong odor. After a few minutes, however, you did not seem to notice the odor at all.

The discharge of mucus that accompanies a severe cold will cause you to lose your sense of smell, because the mucus forms a thick covering over the epithelial cells of the nose and prevents odorous gases from coming in contact with the cells.

The sense of smell is highly developed among a large part of the animal kingdom. These animals use smell as their chief means of learning about their surroundings. In human beings, however, the sense of smell is only mildly developed.

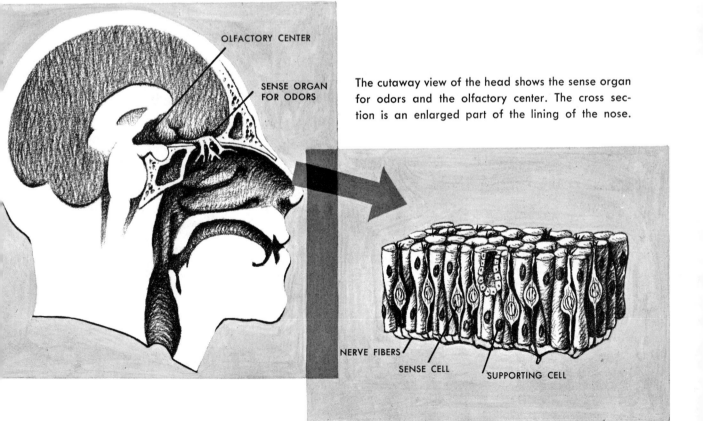

OLFACTORY CENTER

SENSE ORGAN FOR ODORS

The cutaway view of the head shows the sense organ for odors and the olfactory center. The cross section is an enlarged part of the lining of the nose.

NERVE FIBERS

SENSE CELL

SUPPORTING CELL

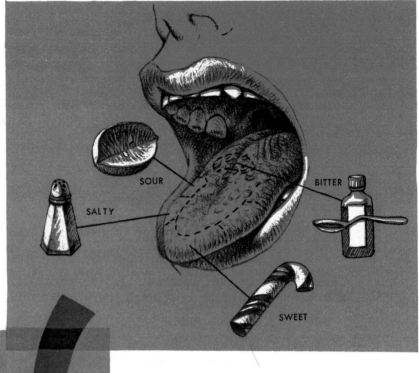

Different taste buds in the tongue are responsible for different taste sensations.

SOUR
SALTY
BITTER
SWEET

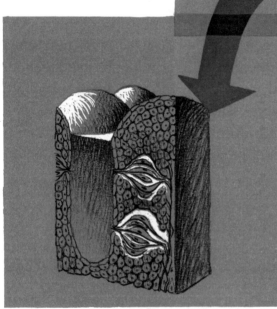

Taste buds are shown in this cross section of tongue.

sations may be divided into *sweet, salty, sour* and *bitter*.

Not all tastes are detected by the same taste buds. Those taste buds at the sides and tip of the tongue transmit impulses of saltiness to the brain. The buds at the tip of the tongue detect sweetness, those near the base detect bitterness and those on the sides detect sourness. Thus, there are certain areas of the tongue in which two kinds of taste buds are located: these are the sides and the tip.

The sense of taste is complicated by the fact that one taste may mask or counteract another. For example, the sweetness of sugar will counteract the sourness of lemon juice.

Taste is further complicated by the fact that certain tastes are actually odors. This is true of the taste of an onion. If a bad cold causes you to lose your sense of smell, you will not be able to taste an onion.

How do we taste things?

Small organs, called *taste buds,* are located just below the surface of the tongue and in three places in the throat. Certain materials taken into the mouth cause taste buds to produce the sensation of taste. Just how this sensation is brought about is not known. Taste, like smell, is probably the result of a mild chemical reaction. Taste sen-

The chief organs of feeling are free nerve endings in the epithelial cells of the body. On the outside of the body, the skin is the organ of feeling; within the body, it is the epithelial cells that line all cavities, such as the mouth, throat, stomach, intestines, ears, chest and sinuses.

How do we feel things?

Not all feelings are detected by the same nerve endings. In the skin there are 16,000 that detect heat and cold and more than four million that detect pain. Still others cause the sensation of touch. This latter sensation is in some way heightened by the hairs of the body. If a hairy portion of the body is shaved, its sensitivity to touch is temporarily reduced.

Sensations of feeling within the body are difficult to explain. Gas that distends the intestine during an attack of indigestion may cause intense pain. Yet surgeons have found that they can cut, burn, pinch and mash the internal organs of a person without causing the patient any pain.

Are all areas of the skin equally sensitive to the touch?

Blindfold yourself. Ask someone to press lightly the blunt point of a pencil on the upturned palm of your hand. Have him repeat this action, using the points of two pencils held about a quarter of an inch apart. Let your helper continue to do this, alternating irregularly between one and two pencil points. As he does this, try to guess how many points are pressing on your hand each time. You will probably make a fairly good score of correct guesses.

But if you repeated this experiment, using the skin of your upper back, close to your spine, you would not be able to tell whether one or two pencil points were being used. This demonstrates that not all areas of the skin are equally sensitive to touch.

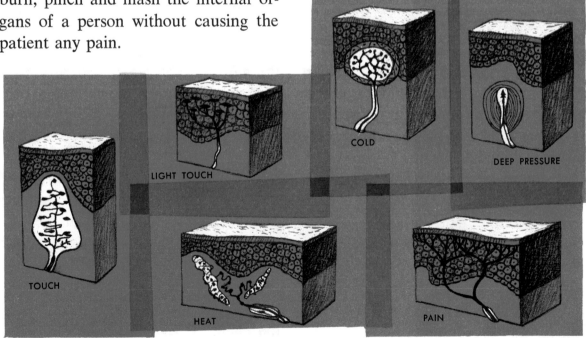

TOUCH

LIGHT TOUCH

COLD

DEEP PRESSURE

HEAT

PAIN

The skin is the organ of feeling. The cross sections show the nerve endings responsible for various sensations.

The Digestive System

We have learned that the blood carries nourishment to the cells of the tissues. This nourishment comes from the food we eat. Certainly, food in the form in which we put it into our mouths could not be carried by the blood. Before food is in a form that enables it to nourish the tissues, it must be greatly changed. This process of change is called *digestion*.

How does the body use food?

The mouth, esophagus (or gullet), stomach, small intestine and large intestine form a continuous tube about thirty feet long called the *alimentary canal*. Food passes through the alimentary canal during the process of digestion. The *liver* and the *pancreas,* two large glands, are also important in the digestion of food. The alimentary canal and these two glands make up the body's *digestive system*.

One of the constituents of food is starch. When food that contains starch is chewed, the saliva in the mouth brings about a chemical change in the starch. As a result of this change, the starch becomes a kind of sugar that is easy for the body to use as nourishment for the cells.

How does digestion begin in the mouth?

A substance, such as saliva, that changes food into a form that can be used by the body is called an *enzyme*. Enzymes are secreted by glands. Saliva is secreted by saliva glands in the roof and floor of the mouth.

Only starch can be digested in the mouth. Fats and proteins, the two other main constituents of food, must be digested farther along in the alimentary canal.

Since food, whether digested in the mouth or other part of the alimentary canal, must be swallowed, the food must first be broken up into small pieces. As we chew, our teeth cut and grind food into small pieces that are wetted by saliva, and finally formed by the tongue into lumps that we can easily swallow.

How do teeth aid digestion?

A tooth is a remarkable structure. The part of the tooth above the gum is the *crown;* below the crown, and covered by the gum, is the *neck;* below the neck is the *root* that lies in the socket of the jaw bone. A tooth has an outside covering of enamel, the hardest material in the body. Inside the enamel, and forming the main part of the tooth, is *dentine.* It looks like bone but is harder. In a cavity in the center of the tooth is the *pulp,* which contains blood vessels and nerves.

When you look on the shelves of a supermarket, you see such a variety of food that it is hard to believe all the different kinds can be divided into a few food elements. But this is true.

What are carbohydrates?

One food element is called *carbohydrate*. Carbohydrates are made up of the chemical elements carbon, hydrogen and oxygen. Starches and sugars, bread and macaroni and rock candy, too, are some carbohydrates. The human body uses carbohydrates as a source of energy. If the body has more carbohydrates than it can use, it may change them into fat, which it stores.

What is fat? Another food element is *fat,* which is a better source of energy than carbohydrate. Butter, margarine, lard and olive oil are a few examples of fat as well as the white irregular streaks in a beefsteak and around the edges of the steak.

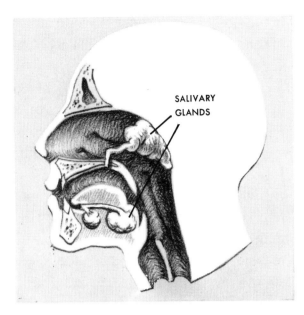

Location of the salivary glands in the human body.

	FOOD SOURCES	BENEFITS FOR BODY	RESULTS WHEN LACKING
A	Yellow and Green Vegetables	Growth — Eyesight	Night Blindness
B₁	Peanuts, Pork	Appetite — Nerves	Poor Appetite
B₂	Liver and Lean Meats	Burns Starches and Sugars	Lip Corners Crack
NIACIN	Wheat Bread — Greens	Healthy Skin	Upset Higher Centers of Brain
C	Strawberries, Red Peppers, Lemon Juice	Healthy Gums	Bleeding Gums
D	Sunshine, Cod Liver Oil	Prevents Rickets	Rickets
PROTEIN	Meat, Kidney Beans, Eggs	Growth	Mental, Physical Inefficiency
CALCIUM	Milk, Swiss Cheese	Formation of Teeth and Bones	Softening of Bones
IRON	Liver, Egg Yolks	Builds Red Blood Cells	Anemia
CALORIES	Butter, Sugar, Wheat Bread	Energy	Fatigue

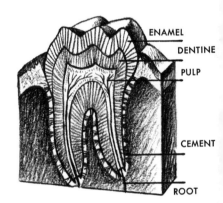

Cross section of a tooth.

ENAMEL
DENTINE
PULP
CEMENT
ROOT

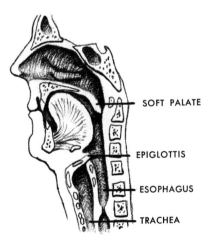

The process of swallowing.

SOFT PALATE
EPIGLOTTIS
ESOPHAGUS
TRACHEA

31

If the body has more fat than it can use for energy, it stores it. That is why some people are stout.

The third main food element is *protein*

What is protein? which is manufactured in the bodies of green plants. When human beings or cattle eat green plants, the plant protein is changed into muscle. When human beings eat meat, which is cattle muscle, they make use of their best source of protein. Meat, also, builds muscle in the human body.

Many foods contain small amounts of

What are vitamins? substances called *vitamins,* which are necessary to the health of the body. Vitamins are named by means of the letters A, B, C, D, and K.

Vitamin A is important for healthy eyes, skin, mucous membranes and for normal growth. Vitamin B is needed for good appetite, good digestion of carbohydrates, normal growth and health of nerves and muscles. Vitamin C is important for growth, the development of teeth, good skin and healing. Vitamin D is needed for strong bones and teeth. Vitamin K is important for the clotting of blood and normal liver function.

Even if we eat enough food, we will not be healthy unless the food contains sufficient vitamins.

Other food elements are called *min-*

What are minerals? *erals.* These are small amounts of certain chemical elements. For example, the elements phosphorus and calcium are needed for healthy teeth and bones.

In order to be healthy, we must give our bodies proper amounts of these food elements. How are we to know just what foods will provide the right amounts? Scientists have worked out the answers, and when our diet includes the proper amounts of each food element, we are then said to be eating a *balanced diet*.

A balanced diet will give the body the nourishment it needs. This is a requirement to maintain good health. A diet that is lacking in certain requirements could lead to a state of unhealth which doctors call *malnutrition.*

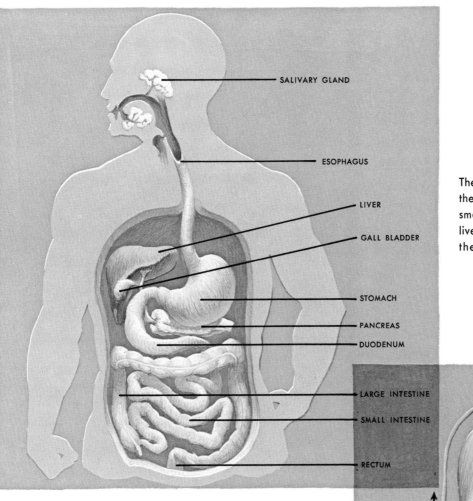

SALIVARY GLAND

ESOPHAGUS

LIVER

GALL BLADDER

STOMACH

PANCREAS

DUODENUM

LARGE INTESTINE

SMALL INTESTINE

RECTUM

The alimentary canal (including the mouth, esophagus, stomach, small and large intestines), the liver and the pancreas make up the body's digestive system.

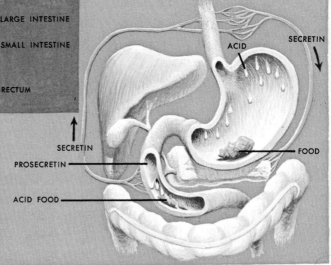

ACID

SECRETIN

SECRETIN

PROSECRETIN

ACID FOOD

FOOD

The stomach and intestine in the digestive process.

Digested food is absorbed through threadlike villi.

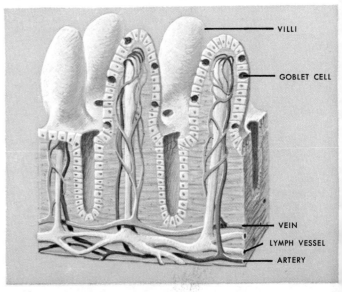

VILLI

GOBLET CELL

VEIN

LYMPH VESSEL

ARTERY

A chicken sandwich, for example, contains starch, fat and protein. The bread is mainly starch, the butter is fat and the chicken is protein.

What is the process of digestion?

When a piece of the sandwich is chewed, the starch is being digested by saliva.

When a mouthful of the sandwich is swallowed, it passes into the *esophagus*. This is the muscular tube that contracts along its length to push the food down into the stomach.

In the stomach, which is a muscle, the food is churned about while digestive juices pour in from glands in the stomach wall. Eventually, the churning action moves food out of the stomach and into the small intestine.

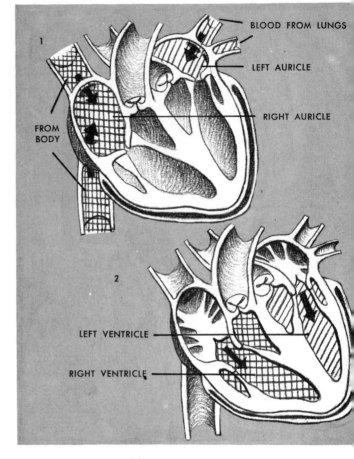

What does the small intestine do? The greater part of the digestive process takes place in the small intestine. Here the protein and the fat are finally changed into forms that can be used by the tissues. The liver contributes to this digestive process by secreting into the small intestine a liquid called *bile*. The pancreas secretes pancreatic juice which further aids in dissolving food.

The small intestine undergoes continual muscular contraction called *peristalsis*. This action pushes the digested food into the large intestine. The surface of the small intestine has a large number of threadlike projections called *villi*. The digested, liquefied food is absorbed through the villi, and passes into capillaries that are inside the villi. Now, the food is in the bloodstream. As we have learned, the blood carries the food to the cells in the tissues, which use the food to provide the body with energy and material for repair.

Not all the parts of the chicken sandwich can be digested. Those parts which are indigestible pass through the large intestine to its lower part, called the *rectum*. Eventually, the indigestible food is eliminated from the rectum through the *anus*.

The Circulatory System

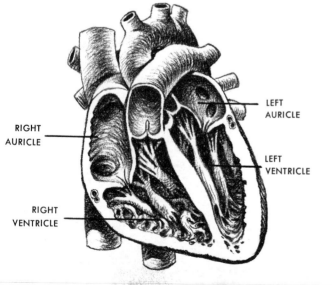

What work does the heart do? Although the study of anatomy is more than 2,000 years old, it was not until the English physician William Harvey described the circulation of the blood, at the beginning of the 17th century, that men knew what work the *heart* did in the body. The heart had been carefully dissected and described, yet no one knew its use.

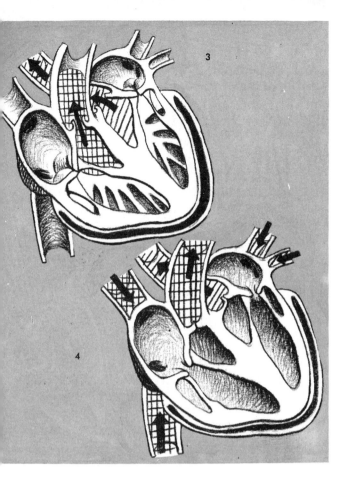

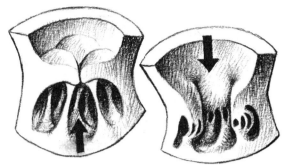

The arrows indicate the direction of blood pressure. Pressure forces closing and opening of the valves.

(1) Auricles contract, squeezing blood into ventricles. (2) Ventricles contract, cuspid valves close, semilunar valves open, blood goes to arteries. (3) Ventricles relax, semilunar valves close, cuspid valves open, blood goes to ventricles. (4) Blood goes to auricles and ventricles, heart relaxes, pauses momentarily.

The heart is a very efficient pump that moves blood through the body. The heart is a muscle that contracts and relaxes about seventy times a minute, for all the minutes of all the years of your life. Each contraction and relaxation of the heart muscle is a *heartbeat*. You have more than 100,000 heartbeats every day. Each heartbeat pumps about two ounces of blood. This results in about 13,000 quarts of blood being pumped each day.

What does the heart look like? The heart is divided into four chambers. The upper two chambers are called *auricles;* the lower two are called *ventricles*. Each auricle is connected with the ventricle below it by a valve that allows blood to flow from the auricle to the ventricle, but not in the opposite direction. The heart also contains a network of nerves that naturally regulates the pumping operation.

A surgeon can replace a seriously ailing heart with a healthy heart taken from a person who has just died. This is called transplanting a heart. Only about half the transplanted hearts work in the new bodies.

It is possible to replace temporarily an ailing heart with one that has nylon muscles, arteries, and veins and stainless steel valves. This heart is attached to a large pumping and electrical control system.

How can you hear a heartbeat? Obtain two small funnels and a length of rubber tubing about one or two feet long. Into each end of the tube, place the snout of one of the funnels.

Now, place the rim of one funnel on the chest of a friend, and place the

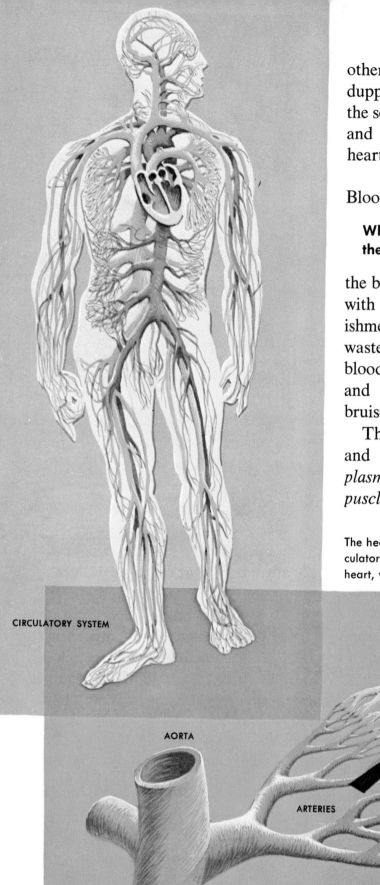

other funnel to your ear. The "lub-dupp, lub-dupp, lub-dupp" you hear is the sound of your friend's heart opening and closing. A doctor listens to the heartbeat by using a stethoscope.

Blood has been called "the river of life." This is an

What work does the blood do?

appropriate description, because the blood supplies the cells of the body with the materials they need for nourishment and repair, and it removes wastes from the cells. In addition, the blood contains cells that fight disease and substances that repair cut or bruised parts of the body.

The blood is made up of both liquid and solid parts. The liquid is called *plasma*. The solid parts are *red corpuscles*, *white corpuscles* and *platelets*.

The heart, blood, veins and arteries make up the circulatory system. The aorta carries the blood from the heart, which branch arteries distribute through body.

CIRCULATORY SYSTEM

VEINS

AORTA

ARTERIES

VEIN

36

The word *corpuscle* is the Latin word for "little body."

More than nine-tenths of the blood consists of red corpuscles. They are so small that a large drop of blood contains more than 250 million of them. They are disc-shaped and concave on each side. These corpuscles contain a substance called *hemoglobin*, which is a compound of iron. Hemoglobin can combine very well with oxygen from the air in the lungs. It is the task of the red corpuscles to carry oxygen to cells in all parts of the body, and upon reaching these cells, to give up the oxygen to them.

What are red corpuscles?

When hemoglobin combines with oxygen, it turns bright red. That is why blood running out of a cut is always red — the hemoglobin is combining with the oxygen of the air.

Red corpuscles live only about fifty to seventy days, and thus, they must be replaced continuously. We learned that the interior of a bone contains reddish tissue, which is due to the presence of red blood cells. Within the marrow of some bones, red cells are formed.

If a person lacks sufficient red cor-

Red corpuscles, white corpuscles and platelets make up the solid part of the blood, as opposed to plasma.

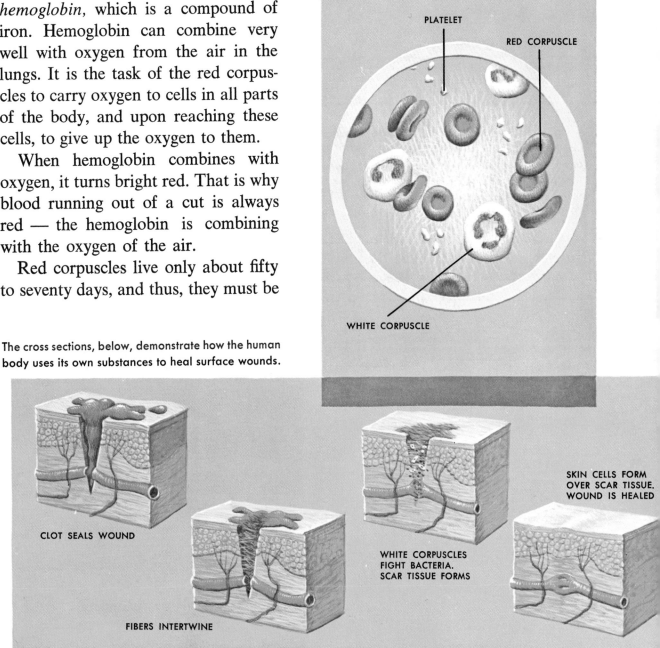

PLATELET

RED CORPUSCLE

WHITE CORPUSCLE

The cross sections, below, demonstrate how the human body uses its own substances to heal surface wounds.

CLOT SEALS WOUND

FIBERS INTERTWINE

WHITE CORPUSCLES FIGHT BACTERIA. SCAR TISSUE FORMS

SKIN CELLS FORM OVER SCAR TISSUE. WOUND IS HEALED

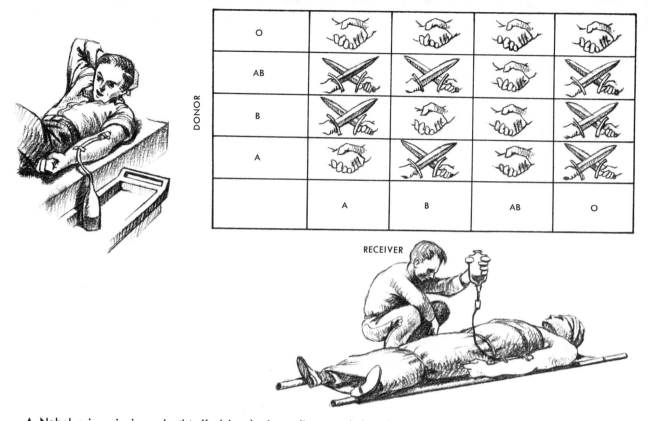

DONOR		A	B	AB	O
	O	🤝	🤝	🤝	🤝
	AB	⚔️	⚔️	⚔️	⚔️
	B	⚔️	🤝	🤝	⚔️
	A	🤝	⚔️	🤝	⚔️
		A	B	AB	O

RECEIVER

A Nobel prize-winning scientist, Karl Landsteiner, discovered that there were four main groups of blood in humans, which he classified as A, B, AB and O. This is important because in a blood transfusion, a person with one kind of blood would become ill if he received another kind that did not agree with him. The chart shows which blood types can be given in transfusion to persons with any of the four blood groups. It also shows the type of blood that persons with any of the four blood groups can receive. The symbol of the handshake stands for "agree with." The crossed swords signify "opposed to." All the races have the same four blood types.

puscles, he is said to have the disease *anemia.* He is usually listless and thin, because his cells do not receive enough oxygen. Some types of anemia may be cured by adding sufficient iron to an anemic person's diet.

How does the blood fight disease? Most white corpuscles are larger than red ones, and there are fewer white corpuscles in the blood than red ones. For approximately every 800 red cells there is only one white cell. White corpuscles have no definite shape, and move about by changing their shape.

Disease is caused by an overabundance of harmful bacteria within the body, and it is the function of the white corpuscles to destroy bacteria. To destroy a bacterium, a white cell moves over to the bacterium and then engulfs it. Once the bacterium is inside the white cell, it is digested.

When large numbers of harmful bacteria invade the blood, the body automatically increases the number of white corpuscles produced by the bone marrow. Then the body has sufficient white cells to destroy most of the invading bacteria.

How does blood clot? You know that when you cut yourself, the blood flows out of the wound for only a short time. Then the cut fills with a reddish solid material. This solid is called a *blood clot.* If blood did

38

not clot, anyone with even a slight wound would bleed profusely. Indeed, the blood of certain persons does not clot, a condition known as *hemophilia*.

The platelets are the particles in the blood responsible for causing it to clot. When blood flows from a cut, it carries platelets. When air comes into contact with the platelets, the oxygen in the air causes the platelets to disintegrate and release a substance that combines with certain substances in the plasma. This combination forms a substance called *fibrin*. Fibrin is in the form of a network of tiny threadlike fibers that trap the cells of the blood to form a dam which holds back the further flow of blood.

Since the heart pumps so much blood,

How does blood move through the body? it must be clear that the same blood must pass through the heart many times in the course of a day. This is true, for the round trip of blood from the heart to distant parts of the body and back takes less than a minute. The round trip to nearer parts of the body takes an even shorter time.

The blood takes two main paths in its trip through the body. When the right ventricle of the heart contracts, blood is forced into a large artery that leads to the lungs. (An *artery* is an elastic tube that carries blood away from the heart.) Here the red cells of the blood take up oxygen from the air in the lungs. They also give up carbon dioxide.

From the lungs, the blood flows through two veins that lead back to the heart. (A *vein* is an elastic tube that carries blood toward the heart.) The blood enters the left auricle and passes through the valve leading to the left ventricle. When the left ventricle contracts, the blood flows into another large artery. This artery branches into smaller arteries that branch several times more into smaller and smaller arteries. The smallest arteries are in the tissues, and are called *capillary* arteries. From the capillaries, the blood transfers nourishment and oxygen to the cells and removes carbon dioxide and other wastes.

Capillary arteries connect with capillary veins. These tiny veins connect with larger and larger veins as they approach nearer to the heart. Blood flowing through the veins eventually reaches a large vein that enters the right auricle of the heart. From the right auricle, the blood flows through the valve leading to the right ventricle, and thus it ends a complete round trip through the body.

The heart, the blood and the veins and arteries make up the body's *circulatory system*.

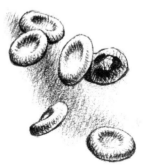

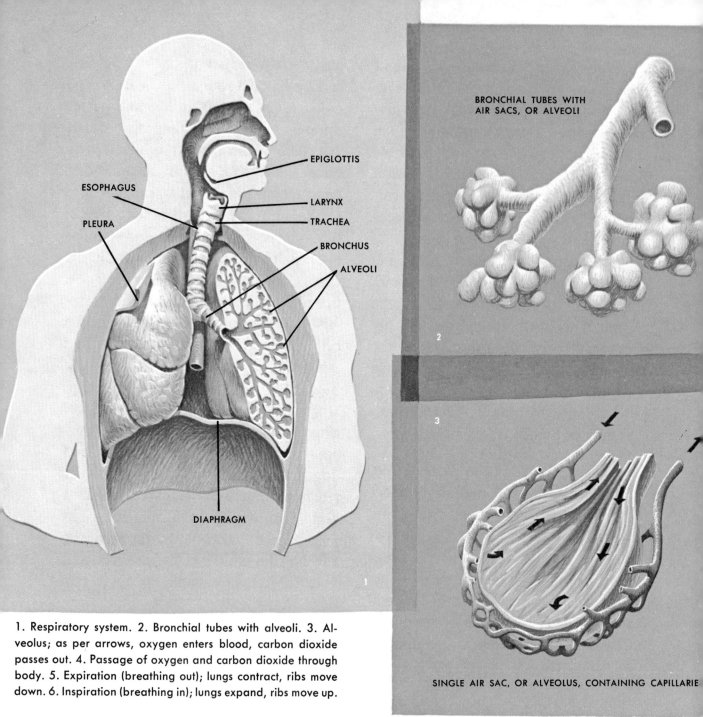

EPIGLOTTIS

ESOPHAGUS

LARYNX

TRACHEA

PLEURA

BRONCHUS

ALVEOLI

DIAPHRAGM

BRONCHIAL TUBES WITH AIR SACS, OR ALVEOLI

SINGLE AIR SAC, OR ALVEOLUS, CONTAINING CAPILLARIE

1. Respiratory system. 2. Bronchial tubes with alveoli. 3. Alveolus; as per arrows, oxygen enters blood, carbon dioxide passes out. 4. Passage of oxygen and carbon dioxide through body. 5. Expiration (breathing out); lungs contract, ribs move down. 6. Inspiration (breathing in); lungs expand, ribs move up.

The Respiratory System

We have learned that the cells of the body need oxygen, and **Why do we breathe?** that the oxygen is obtained from the air. In order to obtain oxygen, we must first get air into our bodies, which we do by inhaling, or breathing in.

Across the body cavity, and below the lungs, is a flat, powerful muscle called the *diaphragm*. When this muscle is moved downward, it causes the ribs to move upward and outward. The result is a partial vacuum that is produced in the lungs. The pressure of the

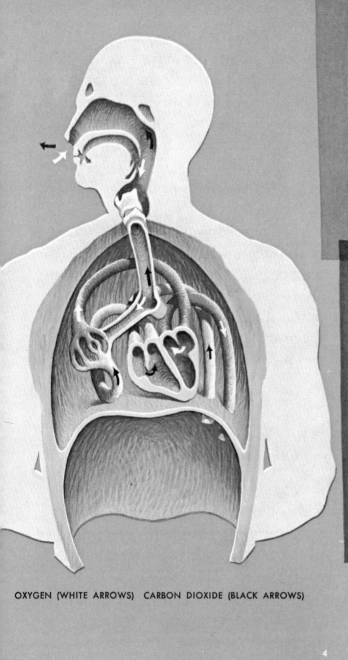

OXYGEN (WHITE ARROWS) CARBON DIOXIDE (BLACK ARROWS)

4

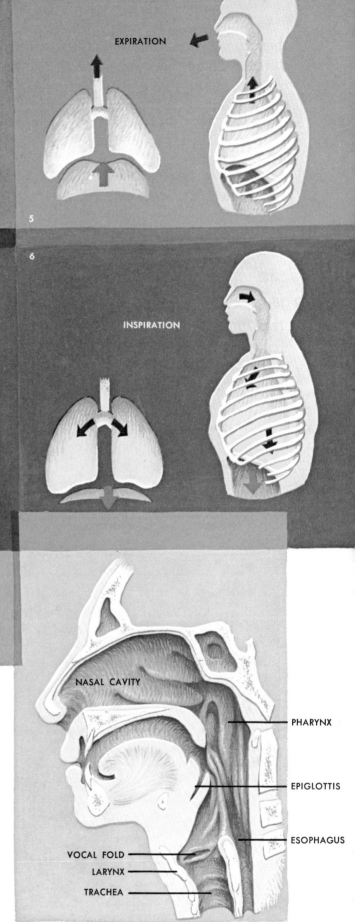

EXPIRATION

5

6

INSPIRATION

NASAL CAVITY

PHARYNX

EPIGLOTTIS

ESOPHAGUS

VOCAL FOLD

LARYNX

TRACHEA

To the right is a cross section of the nasal passage.

air outside the body is now greater than
the pressure in the lungs, and air is
pushed into the nose, down the throat,
through a tube called the *trachea,* and
finally into the lungs.

The trachea divides into two parts,
each entering a lung. Each part is called
a *bronchial tube.* Each bronchial tube
branches many times until the smallest

branches are almost as small as capillaries. These smallest branches are called *alveoli*. The tissues that make up the alveoli contain capillary arteries and veins.

Oxygen passes from the air through the walls of the arteries, and combines with the red blood cells. Carbon dioxide passes through the walls of the veins, and into the air in the lungs.

When the diaphragm relaxes, the ribs move downward, compress the lungs, and force the carbon-dioxide-rich air out of the lungs by the same path through which it entered.

To do this, you must obtain a bell jar,

How can you make a model breathing apparatus?

a one-hole rubber stopper that will fit the jar, a glass tube in the shape of a Y, two small balloons and a large thin piece of rubber.

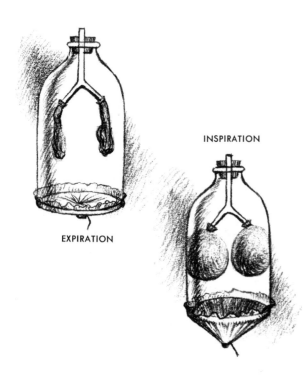

INSPIRATION

EXPIRATION

Place the stopper in the mouth of the jar. Tie the two balloons to the ends of the arms of the Y-tube. Put the other end of the glass tube into the hole in the stopper, doing so by way of the bottom of the bell jar. Tie the large piece of rubber around the bottom of the bell jar.

By pulling downward on the bottom of the large piece of rubber, which represents the diaphragm, you will simulate the breathing process. The upper part of the tube represents the trachea, the arms represent the bronchial tubes, and the balloons represent the lungs.

One way that the cells of the body use

How is air important to the body cells?

the nourishment brought to them by the blood is in providing energy for the body's movements. To provide this energy, certain parts of the nourishment stored in the cells must be combined with oxygen. The oxygen is obtained from the air through the breathing process, and is taken to the cells by the red corpuscles.

When you run you use up more energy.

Why do you breathe more deeply when you run?

This energy must come from the combination of oxygen with the stored nourishment in the cells. The process of combination must take place on a larger scale than usual. To bring this about you need more oxygen in your blood. By breathing more deeply you get more oxygen in your lungs and, thereby, more oxygen in your blood.

The Excretory System

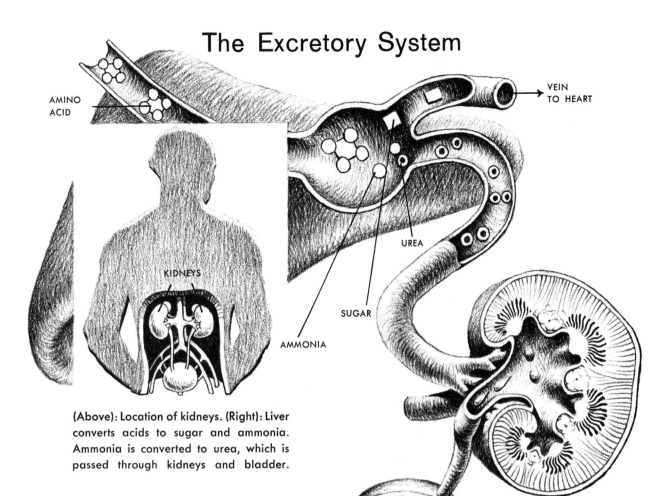

AMINO ACID

VEIN TO HEART

KIDNEYS

UREA

SUGAR

AMMONIA

(Above): Location of kidneys. (Right): Liver converts acids to sugar and ammonia. Ammonia is converted to urea, which is passed through kidneys and bladder.

We have learned that not all of the food we eat is digested. The part not digested is a waste product of the body. Another waste product about which we have learned is the air which contains carbon dioxide.

What does liquid do in the body?

We drink many liquids, some of which provide us with nourishment. Milk is such a liquid. The foods we eat are largely water. The water is quite useful, because, upon entering the bloodstream, it keeps the nourishing food materials dissolved so that they can pass through the membranes of the cells of tissues. It also dissolves waste products within the cells. Somehow, the plasma of the blood, which is partly water, must get rid of the dissolved waste products.

This task is performed by the *kidneys* which are at the lower part of the back, above the hips. Each kidney contains millions of tiny coiled tubes. Blood flows through these tubes and the liquid waste products in the blood are filtered out. These liquid wastes pass from the kidney into a sac where they are temporarily stored. This storage sac is the *bladder*. Every so often, your bladder becomes sufficiently full so as to cause you to want to empty it, a process called *urination*.

How do the kidneys help us?

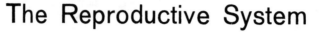

The Reproductive System

ASEXUAL
REPRODUCTION

Living things can reproduce themselves, but nonliving things cannot. A stone can be broken into several pieces; and each piece is permanently smaller than the original stone. Living things reproduce other things that closely resemble the parent. Dogs reproduce themselves as puppies that grow into dogs. Human beings reproduce themseves as babies that grow into adult humans much like their parents.

How do cells reproduce?

The unit of reproduction is the unit of the body — the cell. Within the body, cells are continuously reproducing themselves. After a cell has lived for a certain length of time, changes take place within its cytoplasm. These changes soon cause the cell to begin to narrow at the middle. Eventually, the narrowing process pinches the cell into two cells. But the changes in the cytoplasm have made certain that each new cell has all the parts a cell needs in order to live and function. The new cells soon grow to the size of their parent cell. Then the new cells split in two.

Human and animal reproduction begins with single cells. A female animal has within her body, in a special sac, cells called *egg cells.* A male animal pro-

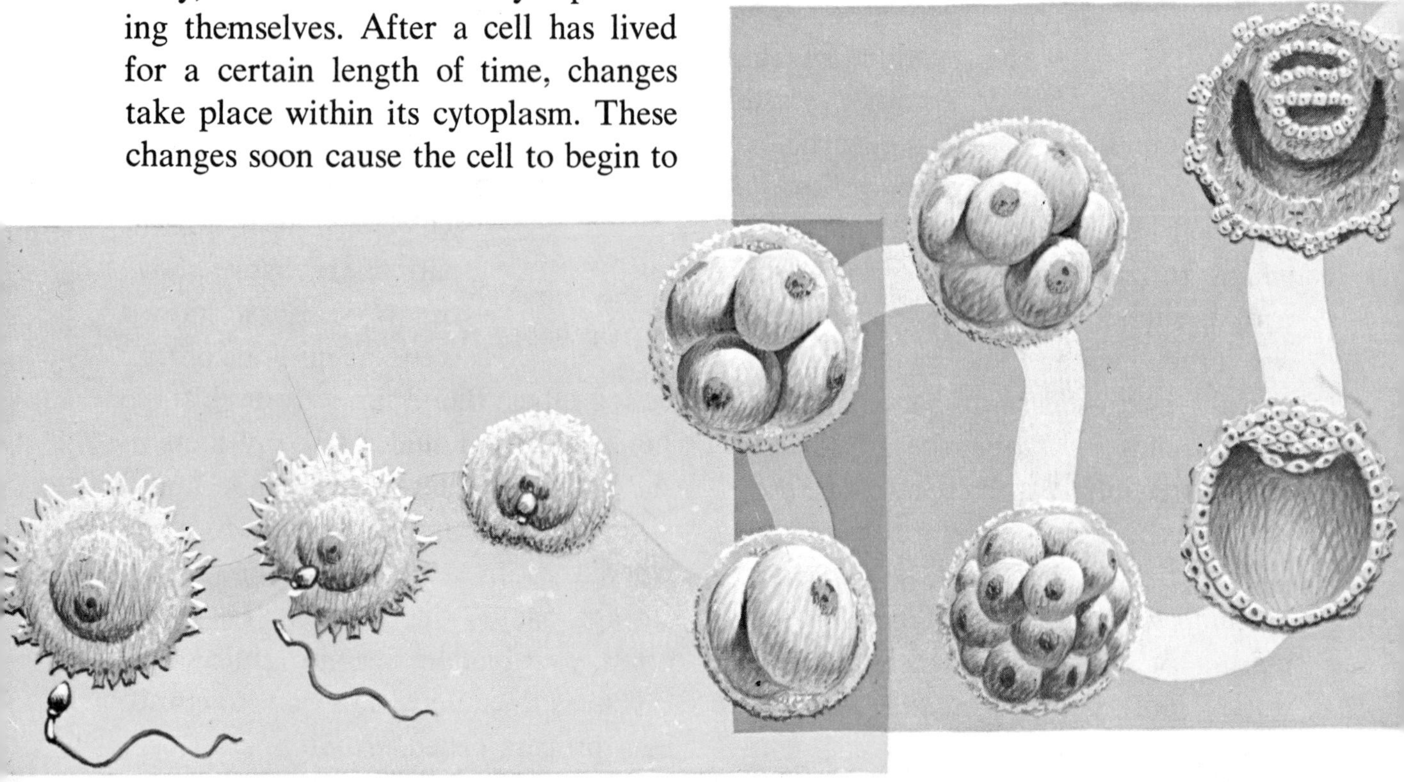

What is the process of reproduction?

44

duces in his body certain cells called *sperm cells*.

If a sperm cell comes in contact with an egg cell, the sperm cell is absorbed by the egg cell. This absorption causes the egg cell to begin to reproduce itself by splitting in two. This splitting process goes on until the original egg cell has become thousands of cells.

These thousands of cells form a hollow ball. As reproduction of the cells in the ball continues, one side of the ball caves inward, creating a double-walled hemisphere.

Up until now, the cells in the hemisphere have all seemed to be of the same kind. Now, as the reproduction of cells continues, different types of

Human beings produce children by the process of reproduction. When a sperm cell, the male sex cell, joins with an egg, the female sex cell, the egg becomes fertilized. The fertilized egg develops into billions of cells that form an embryo, which is the name given to a baby during its first few months of development in the mother's body. Later, the developing infant is called a fetus. It takes about nine months for a child to be born. This nine-month period is known as pregnancy or the gestation period.

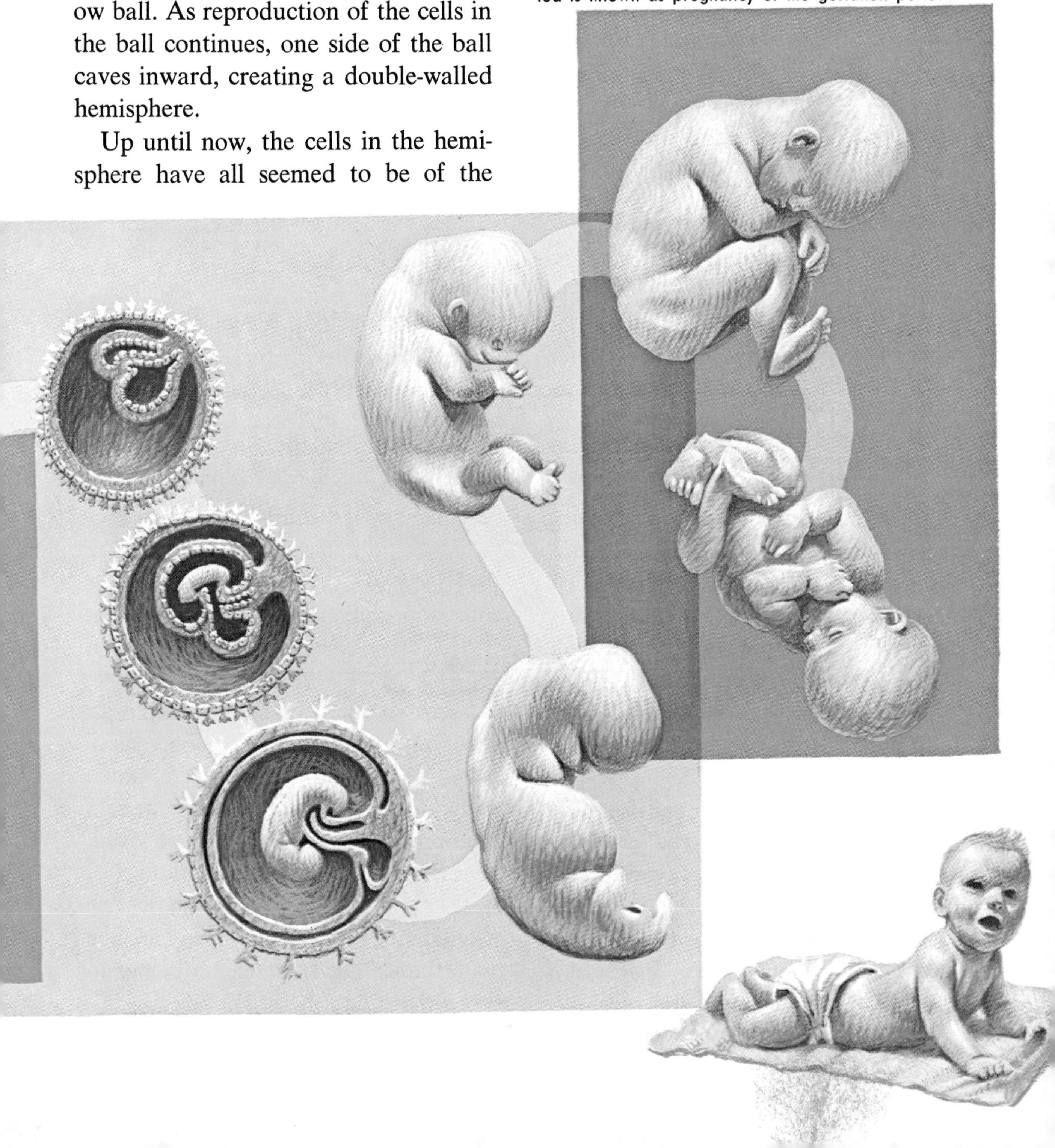

cells form in different parts of the new living thing. In other words, tissues begin to form.

The process of the reproduction of cells in mammals may go on for many months. During this time, what was once a ball of cells begins to form all the parts of the animal's body.

This whole process takes place in the body of the mother animal. The part of her body that holds the newly-forming animal is called the *uterus*. At last, a whole small animal has been formed as the result of continuous cell reproduction. When this time arrives, the muscles of the uterus contract, and the fully-formed little animal is pushed out of the uterus — that is, it is born.

In human beings, the complete process of reproducing a new human being — a baby — takes just a little over nine months.

Your Body and Your Person

We have learned about the parts of the body-machine. When all these parts are put together, we not only have a human body, but also a person.

Why is the human body more than a machine?

What makes us a person is nothing that we can see or touch. It is the fact that we love and want to be loved, have ideas, plan things, daydream, feel sorrow and pity — in short, to do the things that make you human.

Suppose that you and a friend were both hungry, and then you came upon a small amount of food. If you were to act only like a machine satisfying its fuel needs, you would eat all the food yourself. However, since you are a human being, as well as a human machine, you share the food with your friend, even though your fuel needs may not be completely met.

When a machine is fueled, it works until it needs more fuel. The human machine not only does this, but it plans ahead for the time when there will be no more fuel. In other words, human beings know their food will run out, so they plant crops, hunt and fish.

Human beings have *emotions*. It is not easy to say just what an emotion is, but love, hate, sadness, happiness, anger and tenderness are some emotions. All human beings have emotional needs — the need to experience certain emotions. All persons need to be loved, to feel a little bit important, to feel needed and to have new experiences. Attempts to satisfy these needs are the main things that spur human beings to act as they do.

What are emotions?

Care of the Body

Everyone needs some exercise in order to keep the muscles in good condition. When we remember how much of the body is made up of muscles, we realize the importance of this conditioning. The object of exercise is to cause the heart to pump a little faster. This forces a little more blood into capillaries in the tissues, and makes certain that every part of the body is being nourished and having its waste products removed. It also causes deeper breathing, thereby emptying out carbon dioxide from sacs in the lungs that are ordinarily not used.

Need for exercise:

The right amount of exercise gives a feeling of well-being, not fatigue.

Very strenuous exercise or exercising for too long may produce fatigue. Fatigue is caused by wastes accumulating in the body. When muscles are moving continuously or are under strain, they produce more waste products than the body can immediately rid itself of. When this happens, the body needs rest, in order to catch up on waste removal. Sleep is the best kind of rest and one should get enough sleep every day.

Need for rest:

There are many skin diseases, some of which are caused by germs. Others are due to substances to which the skin is very sensitive. For example, boils are caused by an infection of certain bacteria commonly found on the

Care of the skin:

". . . All work and no play makes Jack a dull boy . . ."

skin. Fungus growths can also cause skin diseases. Dirty, neglected skin can result in infestation by insects, such as lice.

A clean skin will either completely eliminate the possibility of these skin ailments, or will lessen the presence of the things that cause them, to the point where the natural protective functions of the body can handle such threats.

The skin should be thoroughly washed with mild soap at least once a day. If an infection or a fungus growth does take place, a physician should be consulted.

The eyes are probably the most valuable sense organs. They should not be exposed to very bright sunlight. In the presence of bright sunlight, sunglasses give adequate protection.

Care of the eyes:

One should always have sufficient

light when reading or writing. Rest the eyes occasionally by looking into the distance or by closing them once in a while.

Never rub the eyes with dirty towels or hands. An infection may result.

The eyes should be tested regularly — at least once a year, or more frequently as the case may be — by an eye doctor.

Above all, never try to treat any eye trouble yourself. Always obtain the help of a physician.

Care of the hair and nails: Those who have healthy skin will probably also have healthy hair and nails. Hair can be kept clean only by washing, and a thorough shampoo once a week is usually sufficient. But if the hair is particularly oily, it may have to be washed more often. Brushing the hair frequently stimulates the circulation in the scalp, and also helps to remove dirt, loose hairs and dandruff.

Most dandruff is not a disease. The outer layer of the skin naturally flakes off, and these flakes may cause mild dandruff. However, if the scalp is also very oily and reddened, it may indicate the kind of dandruff that requires the help of a physician.

If the nails dry and split easily, proper food elements in the diet may be lacking. A balanced diet frequently clears up this condition.

Care of the ears: Never poke any hard object into the ear — it may break the eardrum. Glands in the ear secrete a substance called ear wax. The purpose of this secretion is to keep the eardrum pliable. Sometimes these glands secrete too much wax, which blocks up the ear canal and impairs the hearing. If this happens, do not try to remove the wax yourself. Get the help of a doctor.

Keep the ears clean by washing them with soap and water, and use nothing sharper than a finger to wash in the opening of the ear canal.

Care of the teeth: Particles of food left in the mouth after a meal provide nourishment for bacteria. Bacteria secrete a substance which can dissolve the enamel of the teeth, and thereby cause cavities. For this reason, the teeth should be brushed after each meal whenever possible. This will remove the food particles, and prevent the action of the bacteria.

Since it is not always possible to prevent all decay, even by regular brushing of the teeth, a dentist should be consulted two or three times a year.

The hygienic care of the body becomes especially meaningful when we remember that good health is largely dependent on a body which functions properly. Good health to you all!

THE HOW AND WHY WONDER® BOOK OF
PRIMITIVE MAN

Written by DONALD BARR
Assistant Dean, School of Engineering
Columbia University, New York

Illustrated by MATTHEW KALMENOFF

Editorial Production: DONALD D. WOLF

Edited under the supervision of
Dr. Paul E. Blackwood.
Washington, D. C.

Text and illustrations approved by
Oakes A. White, Brooklyn Children's Museum, Brooklyn, New York

PRICE/STERN/SLOAN
Publishers, Inc., Los Angeles
1985

Introduction

This *How and Why Wonder® Book* deals with a question that is perplexing and fascinating — "Where did man come from?" The book relates how scientists use the records of "prehistory" to help answer this question. It throws light on various theories about how man developed from primitive beginnings to a creature who first used simple tools and then more complex ones. It reminds us that after thousands of years, man began speaking and writing and, with these skills, history had begun.

The How and Why Wonder® Book of Primitive Man reveals how different kinds of scientists — archaeologists, anthropologists, geologists and others — combine their discoveries and knowledge to fill in the gaps with information that is needed to get a clearer picture of early man. We learn, too, how it is that there are people of many different kinds and appearances in the world today. Yet we see, also, that men everywhere probably have a common ancestry and that all men are "brothers under the skin." At no other time in history has it been so important for people everywhere to possess attitudes favorable to understanding each other.

This book can help parents, teachers and children to build sound knowledge by supplying up-to-date information on common questions about man's origins.

Paul E. Blackwood

Dr. Blackwood is a professional employee in the U. S. Office of Education. This book was edited by him in his private capacity and no official support or endorsement by the Office of Education is intended or should be inferred.

ISBN: 0-89434-076-X (set)

Science Library © 1987 J.G. Ferguson Publishing Company
Chicago

Contents

The New Animal

There was a new kind of animal in the forest . . .

The wild dogs found a strange scent and followed it through the thick bushes and along the pebbly banks of the rivers, until, in the cold of the night, they came to an open hillside. And there, crouching in the hollow under a hanging cliff, were the Invaders. They were like no other animals the dogs had ever seen, and there were many of them in the pack, and their strong smell excited the dogs, standing back among the trees, fur bristling and mouths dripping. The new animals would make a good fight and a good feast! But in the midst of the Invader pack there was . . . Something Else. It was just as if a little puddle of daylight had been left behind when the night fell. And in the center of that light-puddle was a snapping, dancing thing. It was the color of the sun and hot like the sun — Fire. So the dogs turned and ran back into the dark woods. Only when they were alone with their hunger under the sheltering leaves did they lift up their muzzles and howl.

The next day, a saber-toothed tiger watched the Invaders coming through the trees. How noisy they were, these new animals! They made loud grunting and chattering sounds with their mouths, and they tore their way recklessly through the bushes, as if there were no other animals in the forest. They walked in a clumsy way, straining up on their hind legs. Their strange, flat, front paws seemed to be of no use in walking, and just hung down or pushed aside the branches. The creatures seemed to have almost no claws at all. They had long dirty manes, but the rest of their fur was poor and thin. However, they were biggish animals and bulged with meat, and the tiger thought that if it charged them suddenly, the whole foolish, brawling herd would run away in fright, and it could feast on the first one that fell. So the tiger chose its prey — a female carrying her cub. Its great mouth yawned open in a snarl of joy, its long, curving upper teeth flashed, and it leaped. But it was a bad leap. The tiger's claws only raked the creature's flesh, and she gave a high scream. And instead of plunging into the bushes to escape, the whole herd turned to their wounded member. It was then that the tiger saw The Claw. One of the Invaders raised his front paw as he ran, and now it looked weak and useless no longer, for the tiger saw there was a strange, straight, gray toe growing from it — long and terrible — and The Claw buried itself in the tiger's throat, and the tiger died.

Even the mastodon, with its fearsome tusks and its curling powerful trunk that could pull up a young tree, was helpless before the Invaders. A little band of the new animals found a bull mastodon in the forest. A great lord of the herd it was — all the animals of the forest walked softly when it was near. But these creatures picked up rocks and pieces of trees in their strange clever forepaws and threw them at the mastodon so that its little eyes reddened with

Early man developed the use of fire, which made him master of the animal kingdom.

fury and it charged them, trumpeting. Then they ran before it. Screeching figures like big featherless birds they were. They dodged this way and that and led the mastodon on and on. And then . . . it stepped on what had looked like ordinary leaves and twigs, yet the ground gave way under it. And there was a deep pit underneath the leaves, and it crashed down, and in a moment the vicious animals were upon the mastodon, slashing at it with tree branches that had sharp stones growing on them, and the victim was dead.

Here is one of the Invaders, squatting on the pebbly edge of the river. His heavy, almost hairless shoulders are hunched forward; his tangled head is cocked downward watchfully; his hand clutches a stout, sharp twig. There is no sound except the gurgle of the stream dashing and whirling between the

4

stones. There is no movement except the flash of the sunlight on the water and the glitter of the creature's eyes as they peer this way and that into the speckled depths . . . A streak of movement! The creature's hand shoots out, and a fish is pinned to the bottom of the stream by the stick. The creature seizes the squirming fish with his other hand, pulls it out — and begins to eat it.

He stands up. Look at him. He is an ugly fellow. He stands only a little over five feet tall, but the upper part of his body is large. His neck is thick. His shoulders slump forward heavily. His matted chest bulges out in a great curve. His arms are fairly long, but they look longer because his legs are thick and bowed and very short, and he seems to be keeping his knees slightly bent. Under the shaggy hair, his head is large, but you have to look carefully to see this, because he has a way of pushing his face forward so that the back of his head sinks down between his shoulders. He has a big face. He has immense brow-ridges jutting out above his suspicious eyes. His forehead is very low and sloping. He has an enormous jaw — which he grinds forward and backward in a strange way as he chews the fish — but he has almost no chin.

Look hard at him. He is the new master of the forest. There is no animal he cannot kill. With these strange, clever front paws of his — his hands — he is going to sew and knot together their skins to provide warmth and shelter for himself, partly defeating even the greatest and oldest of his enemies, the cold and the storm. With the powerful brain behind that low forehead, this animal is going to change other animals, making them serve and obey him. This forest where he now stands spitting out fish bones and peering into the shadows for his enemies, this vast forest will be cut down, and in its place he will build a great city. That brain of his will perhaps think of fantastic crimes, things too bloody for a saber-toothed tiger, but that brain of his will also think of fantastic beauty, of sounds that will make your heart race in your chest, of shapes and colors that will stop the breath in your nostrils . . .

He still has such a long way to go! But he has come far already. He himself does not know how far. No one in the Invader band remembers when they started, or where. Always they have been on the move. They hunt in a place until there are no more deer or dogs or horses, and they gather berries and nuts until the branches are bare, and then they start out again through the forests. Their mothers and fathers before them were wanderers all their lives — from hill to hill, from river to river, from winter cave to winter cave.

This is a brave band. It has gone up to the very edge of the Cold, to where almost all the trees are dead and none of the other animals will go, except the reindeer. Some of the bravest have even seen the Moving Mountain itself. This one saw it. It is a great wall of ice reaching up and up into a sky that is filled with snow, and when he listened he could hear the mountain crawling along the ground, making terrible noises as if the earth were groaning with pain. It crawled too slowly to see, but on the cruel white face of the mountain he could see where it had picked up huge stones and trees and devoured them.

The old ones in the band tell stories at the campfire. They tell of other kinds of places — of lands where it is always summer, of lands where there are strange beasts almost like themselves but living in trees, of rivers so wide that no one can see the other side, and of lands of death where there is no water and no grass. These places are many winters away, many lives away. But the band has been there . . .

The stories of the old ones are true, and so are many stories the oldest of the old don't know. For this creature is a Man, and the story of Man is so long that no one could tell it all, and so astonishing that no one would believe it all. That story began with dust out in the freezing space between the stars. It took place in the boiling rock of the volcanoes, in great clouds of gas and great lightning-storms that lasted millions of years, in the slime at the bottom of oceans, in mud, in treetops. It took place in bits of strange chemicals too small to see, and in murderous giant lizards. We ourselves know only a little of the story, and most of what we know we have had to guess, using the brain we have inherited from that strange creature in the forest . . .

And so the new animal, the Man, finishes eating his fish, spits out a bit of fin, and lumbers off to his lair.

Before History

About fifty centuries ago, writing was

What does "prehistoric" mean?

invented so people could put things down on clay or stone or animal skin or paper if they thought it might be important to remember them. Anything that is important to people is a part of history. So we may say that written history is about 5,000 years old.

But there have been people — people who were more or less human — on the earth for about 500,000 years. So ninety-nine percent of the time that human beings have been on this planet was *before written history,* and that earlier time we call "prehistoric." "Pre" is just Latin for "before."

Scientists think that man's wonderful

When did prehistory start?

story really begins long before there were any men. Man arrived on earth very late, and he probably didn't come suddenly. It seems quite clear that he slowly developed — we say that he "evolved" — from a much more primitive form, perhaps even from a very different kind of creature. In other words, your ancestors thousands, perhaps millions of years ago looked and acted very different from you. But every once in a while there were some children who were a little different from their parents, a little smarter or taller or less hairy. And these tiny improvements kept up over thousands and thousands of years until you came along.

Some people even believe that those old ancestors of yours may even have evolved in that same way from another kind of animal, and that kind from another, and that from another, and that from another. But this knowledge is still hidden, farther back into prehistory than we can see yet. Perhaps if we could only find enough facts, we could carry man's history all the way back to when the earth itself was formed, about 4,500,000,000 years ago!

Although there are no written records

How do we find out about prehistory?

that come to us from before the year 3000 B.C., there are other kinds of records. They do not use words but they tell us a lot.

Big events are not neat. In a war, for instance, the general's mother does not come and tidy up the battlefield afterward. So bullets or arrows are left around, and long, long afterward an expert on bullets or arrows may find one and say, "Ah! This bullet is the kind used in such-and-such a gun. And that gun was the kind used by such-and-such an army at such-and-such a time. Now, what was *that* army doing here?" And if he finds some bullets used by the other side in the battle, he may begin to figure out what happened in the war. And yet there might be no written records of that battle at all.

Or perhaps a tribe of Indians decides to move to a new hunting ground. They bundle up their belongings, roll up their tents, load their horses and set out. But of course they leave a lot of junk behind — worn-out things, or stuff too heavy to carry. And many years later an expert on Indians may come and say, "Ah! Such-and-such Indians once lived here. Here is a blanket with their design. We never knew *they* came this far south."

Graves are very important. Even if there are no gravestones, even if there are no clothes or favorite possessions buried with the dead, even if there is nothing but just bones, an expert on skeletons can learn a great deal. He can probably tell how long ago the people lived. He can tell how old each person was when he died. He might say, "Ah! These people lived around 3700 B.C. But see how this skull was cut open and grew back again — they must have known how to do some brain surgery even *then*!"

Such records are not complete. Often they are like puzzles that scientists must guess and argue about.

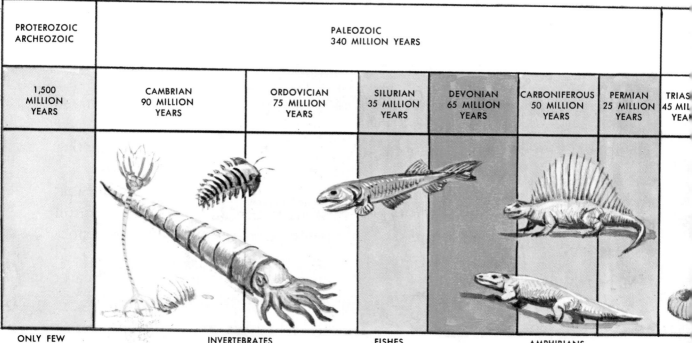

PROTEROZOIC ARCHEOZOIC	PALEOZOIC 340 MILLION YEARS						
1,500 MILLION YEARS	CAMBRIAN 90 MILLION YEARS	ORDOVICIAN 75 MILLION YEARS	SILURIAN 35 MILLION YEARS	DEVONIAN 65 MILLION YEARS	CARBONIFEROUS 50 MILLION YEARS	PERMIAN 25 MILLION YEARS	TRIAS 45 MIL YEA

ONLY FEW FOSSILS FOUND   INVERTEBRATES   FISHES   AMPHIBIANS

Early man used primitive but deadly weapons as he hunted the mastodon, an ancestor of the elephant.

Dozens of different kinds of scientists can tell us things about prehistoric times. When we want to know about how the earth **Who are the experts on prehistory?** formed, we go to the *astronomers* (Greek for "star-lawyers"), who study stars and planets; and we go to the *physicists* (Greek for "nature-followers"), who study the forces and particles that form the atom; and we go to the *chemists* (Greek for "juice-pourers"), who study how atoms behave. Of course, they have no records at all of what happened 4,500,000,000 years

There is something wrong with this picture. A dinosaur could not have chased a man, for as we know, dinosaurs were already extinct when man emerged.

The chart is a record of life on earth as told in its rocks. It is divided into eras, which are divided into periods, and shows the form of life dominant in each phase of the earth's geological history. You can see how late is man's appearance on the earth. All figures in the chart signify duration of time.

...ZOIC ...ILLION YEARS		CENOZOIC 70 MILLION YEARS		
...SSIC ...LION ...RS	CRETACEOUS 60 MILLION YEARS	PALEOCENE to PLEISTOCENE 70 MILLION YEARS		RECENT
...OSAURS			MAMMALS	MAN

ago. But from studying how things work now, they can tell us how things might have worked then.

If we want to know when things happened on earth, and what the earth was like when different animals were evolving, we go to the *geologists* (Greek for "talkers about the earth"), who study rocks and soils.

When we want to know what animals evolved, we go to the *paleontologists* (Greek for "talkers about ancient beings"), who study the buried bones and tracks of animals of the past. And when we want to know how animals evolved, we go to the *geneticists* (Greek for "birth-followers"), who are trying to find out why we are like our parents and sometimes not quite like them.

When we want to know about human bones, we go to the *physical anthropologists* (Greek for "talkers about what man is made of"), who learn about the human body. When we want to know about the tools and ornaments that belonged to prehistoric men, we go to the *archeologists* (Greek for "talkers about ancient things"), who study all the objects made and used by people in past ages.

For instance, you will often see cartoons showing cave men being chased by dinosaurs. But this could never have happened. The physical anthropologists tell us which bones are the bones of the prehistoric men who lived in caves. The paleontologists tell us which bones are the bones of the giant reptiles. The geologists tell us that the human bones come from layers of earth that are 50,000 years old, and the dinosaur bones come from rocks 150,000,000 years old.

How do we find the records of the past?

Almost all the bones, tools, weapons and ornaments that tell us what men were like and how they lived in the distant past are buried in the ground. Many have been found by accident. But most of the records of the past still lie beneath the surface of the earth, waiting to be discovered.

How do the records of the past get buried?

Fortunately for science, man is a messy animal. In the last hundred years or so, some people in some places have learned that dirt breeds germs and germs cause disease — so they have gone in for cleanliness and garbage disposal. But the old way of doing things was just to throw rubbish away and leave it. When a prehistoric man finished gnawing on a bone, he tossed it on the ground. When he killed a handsome animal and scraped down its skin to make a new suit for himself, he dropped the old skin — it became

BATON

PAINTED PEBBLES

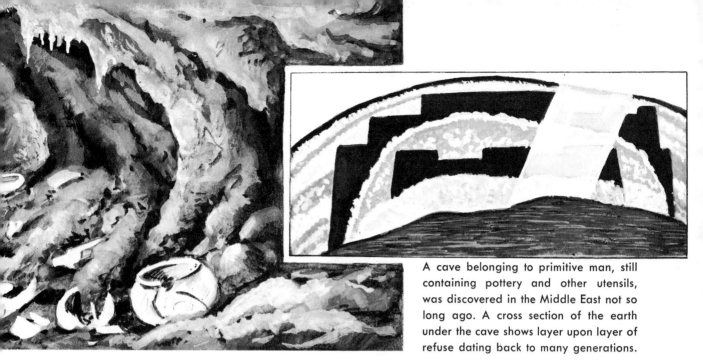

A cave belonging to primitive man, still containing pottery and other utensils, was discovered in the Middle East not so long ago. A cross section of the earth under the cave shows layer upon layer of refuse dating back to many generations.

a rug or a bed. When he broke a stone tool, he kicked the pieces out of the way. When he died, he might well have been rolled onto the trash heap with the other old bones.

Wherever man lived in caves, the floor was covered with stinking trash. People trampled it into the dirt and tracked mud over it, and as layer after layer of this refuse was added, the cave floor slowly rose. The tribe would leave. The cave would be empty, or bears would live in it. The garbage on the floor would rot away until only bones and stone chips were buried in black dirt. A new tribe would come and a new layer would start. Scientists have dug out caves where these floor layers went down sixty feet.

Where men lived outdoors, or in lean-tos made of tree branches and animal hides, rains and floods would wash sand and gravel over the old campsites, or landslides would bury them. Roving bands of prehistoric men were slaughtered by enemies, and their bodies were left for the animals, and the leaf-mold

and forest growth slowly covered the bones. Villages and even cities were abandoned, or burned, or sacked, and new towns were built on the leveled ruins. When Heinrich Schliemann dug up the city of Troy, he found nine Troys, one above the other.

The whole record of life, long before man, is kept in the same way. As thousands of thousands of years have passed since life first began on this planet, vast, slow surges in the earth's molten core have shifted the rocky crust of the world. Continents rose from the oceans. Great seas swirled into the collapsing plains. Lakes dried up. Rivers cut deep canyons in the soil and stone. In these changes, life and death went on. Wherever water has laid down beds of soil or sand or gravel or rock formed from hardened mud, scientists can dig down and go back in time — the topmost layers which record the Age of Man, and then down into ancient layers where the bones and shells of strange animals that vanished millions of years ago silently tell their story.

11

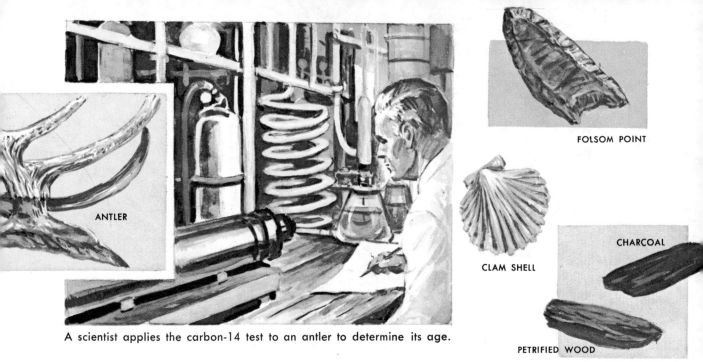

ANTLER

FOLSOM POINT

CLAM SHELL

CHARCOAL

PETRIFIED WOOD

A scientist applies the carbon-14 test to an antler to determine its age.

How do we know how old things are?

In reading the long story told to us by the traces that living creatures have left in the earth, it is usually not hard to tell which plants or animals lived before or after others. As we go down into a series of layers of rock, or gravel, or packed mud, we know that the deeper the layer, the older it is. In many parts of the world, there are series of layers that are very much alike. The same little shells or animal bones are embedded in layers of the same kind of rock or earth. Many of these are kinds of animals that died out after a while. So we can guess that a certain layer in America was laid down at the same time as a certain layer in Europe. And slowly we can build up a kind of list, in the proper order, of all the things that took place in each part of the world for millions of years — the floods and droughts, the kinds of animals, the kinds of men.

But even when we know the order in which things happened, it is hard to tell just how long ago they happened. Until a few years ago, scientists really had to guess how long it took rocks to form or mud to pile up. But now they have invented some strange and ingenious ways of finding the "dates" of ancient layers of the records of the past.

Several new methods of "dating" depend on tiny clocks hidden inside the atoms of certain substances. For instance, practically all the chemicals that living things are made of contain a certain kind of atom called the carbon atom. And there is one form of carbon atom that is special: it is a little heavier than the ordinary carbon atom, and it is "radioactive" — that is, it falls apart by itself after a while and turns into another kind of atom. This kind of carbon is called carbon-14, and it falls apart at a steady rate which never changes. If there were 10,000 atoms of regular carbon and 100 atoms of carbon-14 in a certain piece of bone in 3600 B.C., then there are 10,000 atoms of regular carbon and only 50 atoms of carbon-14 in that piece of bone today.

CROSS SECTION
THROUGH LAYERS
OF ROCK

DINOSAUR FOOTPRINTS

CROSS SECTION OF TREE
GUTTED BY FIRE

CROSS SECTION
OF TREE
IN NORMAL CONDITION

OSS SECTION
LEANING TREE

Each year, tree-trunks grow thicker by adding a new layer of wood just under the bark. In dry weather, the layers are thin; in wet weather, they are thick. By measuring the thickness of the rings, you can make a year-by-year history of the weather from the time the tree started to grow. You can match the outside ring of a dead tree with the inside ring of a living one and carry the weather-history back a hundred years more. An older tree, dead and buried, will give the weather-history of earlier centuries. The age of wood found in the diggings can be determined by looking at the tree-ring weather-history for the part of the world where it was dug up. And that will tell you when the wood layers were formed.

Now it happens that carbon-14 atoms only get into animals, along with regular carbon atoms, while the animals are alive. So scientists have invented wonderful ways of counting these tiny atoms — so tiny they cannot be seen even with the most powerful microscope — and comparing the different kinds of carbon atoms to figure out how long ago the animal died. In great laboratories filled with gleaming tangles of glass tubing and flashing lights and the whir and click of the atom-counters, scientists can test a little crumb of bone and say:

"This man died 75,000 years ago."

Where Did Man Come From?

Where did living things come from?

The story of the earth began in the terrible cold of empty space. This is how many scientists think it happened — or *could* have happened: Where our sun and the earth and the other planets now are, there was once only a vast dark cloud of dust and gas. Slowly, gently, the light from the stars around it pushed this material together. Then the pull of gravity squeezed it together harder and harder and harder. In the center, a lump formed, and its gravity pulled more and more material in, and finally it got so big that the atoms in the center of it were squashed by the tremendous weight of the material around them. This started a wild flare-up of nuclear energy, like an endless hydrogen bomb explosion, and soon the lump was a huge glowing ball — the sun.

Around it the rest of the dust cloud wheeled and swirled, and little whirl-

13

pools of dust began to form, and they too became lumps, and these formed glowing hot planets and their moons.

When the third planet from the sun — the one we call Earth — cooled a little, it had a soft wrapping of air around it, but not the air we breathe. If you had tried to breathe the air of the newborn earth, you would have choked to death in a few seconds. It was made of certain gases — hydrogen, methane, ammonia and water vapor. For millions of years, there were terrific storms all around the earth, and great flashes of lightning sizzled through the clouds. And for millions of years, the sun's rays beat down. The electricity and the rays rearranged the atoms of the gases into strange acids called "amino acids," which are the building blocks that your flesh and blood are made of. Here and there, the floating amino acids combined into the right arrangements, and tiny bits of "protein" were formed. Protein is not quite alive.

And at last some other acids, even more wonderful, were formed. They were "nucleic acids," and when these atom-groups, or molecules, were linked together in a certain way, other acid stuff stuck to them *and arranged itself next to them in the same pattern.* These were the first living things.

All living creatures are members of the same great family. That idea is called "the theory of evolution." The lion, the giraffe, the worm, the

What is evolution?

eagle, the sparrow and the wasp are all cousins. Scientists believe that their first ancestor was one "cell," floating in the stormy oceans of the earth two billion years ago. It was a tiny cluster of proteins with a special corkscrew-shaped set of the wonderful nucleic acids in the middle of it. This middle part of the cell picked up bits of chemical from the acids in the protein-sack around it, and arranged them into a copy of itself. Then the copy split off from the original and separated. It pulled part of the protein cluster with it and became the center of a new cell. Then both cells split. So there were four cells. Then eight. Then sixteen. And soon there were billions of cells, each containing a perfect copy of the nucleic-acid corkscrew.

Gradually these cells began to change. They became specialists. Some specialized in producing one kind of chemical, others produced other kinds. Some changed shape when an electric current touched them. Others were electrified when light hit them. And these specialist-cells no longer lived by themselves. They lived in groups or colonies, and divided the different kinds of work between them.

These colonies copied themselves, too. But it was not as if a football team went out and organized another football team, with the quarterback picking the new quarterback and the left tackle picking the new left tackle. It was rather as if there were a master plan for the colony, written down in nucleic

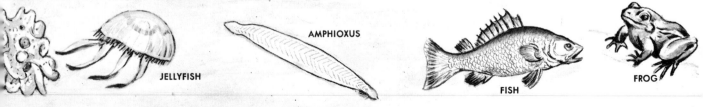

AMOEBA

JELLYFISH

AMPHIOXUS

FISH

FROG

acids. Each cell had a copy. And a copy was kept in a special cell to give to the new colony.

Then the master plans changed little by little, and the colonies became more and more complicated. The cells that were sensitive to light began to be the eyes of the colony. The cells that gave off electricity were the nerves. Some of the chemical work-cells were the stomach. And now there were animals.

As soon as scientists — these were the geneticists, the "birth - followers" —discovered that each animal had a master plan that was passed on from animal to animal, they had a big problem to solve. If the designs were just copied over and over, how could the animals ever change?

How do different animals evolve?

After all, their friends the paleontologists—the "talkers about ancient beings" — could show them plenty of animal skeletons which proved that there *had* been changes. Animals had gotten bigger, or gotten smaller, or changed shape.

If an animal had a father and a mother, its design would be a sort of mixture of its parents — and sometimes a bit of its grandparents, too. That would explain how one horse might be different from another horse. But it would not explain how, in a few million years, all the horses lost their toes and got hoofs.

Changes in the plan of an animal are called "mutations"—which is just Latin for "change." And scientists say that little accidents are happening all the time to the acids of the master plan. For instance, there are rays from outer space that are always shooting through us. Parts of the acid-stuff might get shifted around by these "cosmic rays." Mostly these accidents just spoil the copy of the plan so badly that it cannot be used, but once in a while an accident makes a change that can really work.

And what you are is a collection of millions and millions of such changes, in the form of a colony of fifty trillion cells.

Not all changes are good. If a mutation is extremely different, then the little creature may not live long enough to be born. But new and different offspring are always being born in the great family of living creatures—among men as well as among other living things.

What is natural selection?

MAN

NEANDERTHAL

GORILLA

MULE DEER

Scientists believe that the development of life on earth began with one-celled animals. After two billion years, man emerged.

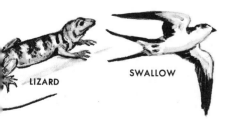

LIZARD

SWALLOW

15

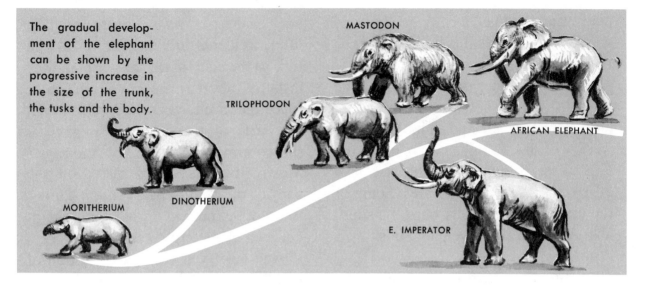

The gradual development of the elephant can be shown by the progressive increase in the size of the trunk, the tusks and the body.

MASTODON

TRILOPHODON

AFRICAN ELEPHANT

MORITHERIUM

DINOTHERIUM

E. IMPERATOR

If the mutation makes the animal weaker, it is more likely to get killed in a fight, or to die of sickness or hunger. It will not live as long and have as many children as its ordinary brothers. So the old plan will be carried on and the new one will die out.

If the mutation makes the animal stronger or more clever, it will win its fights and eat well, and the animal will probably live long and have many children to carry on the new master plan.

This is called the "natural selection" of mutations, and it means that the master plan of animals is always slowly changing to fit the world they have to live in. For example, drugs such as penicillin used to be wonderful at killing germs, including the terrible staphylococcus microbes that cause infections. Doctors gave penicillin to practically everybody for practically everything. So the staphylococcus microbe had to live in a world full of penicillin. And now many staphylococcus microbes have a mutation that keeps them unharmed by penicillin.

The same thing seems to have been happening to men. That is why you have longer legs than the fellow we met in the forest in the first chapter.

How did the giraffe get its neck?

There used to be a great argument among scientists about how giraffes got their long necks. For the skeletons of ancient giraffes showed that once upon a time they had short necks. And this is an important question. Because you got your excellent brain the same way the giraffe got its long neck.

Some scientists claimed the giraffes had lived by eating the leaves off the trees and after a while, when they had eaten all the leaves from the lower branches, they had to stretch their necks to get at their food. They stretched so hard that their necks grew a little longer, and their children were born with longer necks, which they stretched still more. So *their* children were born with still longer necks, and so on and so on. In other words, these scientists said that if your body changes, the same change will take place in your master plan.

Other scientists said this was nonsense. They said that nothing that happened to your body would make any change in your master plan. The giraffes ate all the leaves off the lower branches. But some giraffe-families happened to be born with longer necks than others, just as in some people-families everyone has a longer nose than in some other families. This had nothing to do with stretching. It was because of little shifts in the acids of the master plan. However, the giraffe-families that did have longer necks got more to eat. They were healthier and had a better chance to get away from lions and other giraffe-eaters. So the long-neck families had more children than the short-neck families. The long-neck mutations won because they were better tree-eaters and there were not quite enough trees to go around.

They were right. These scientists, led by the great naturalist, Charles Darwin, said that *man evolved because his powerful brain helped him to stay alive.*

When Darwin's books on evolution

Do all people believe the theory of evolution?

were printed a hundred years ago, many people said Darwin did not believe in God's plan, but in a horrible universe run by lucky accidents and greedy fighting. They said he was making man out to be nothing more than a smart ape. But these people need not have worried. The theory of evolution says certain things happened. It does not say, and it could not say, *why* those things happened. If God made the world and runs the world, then evolution *is* God's plan. And it is a majestic and beautiful plan. With evolution, even accidents are part of the plan of life, and even the lowest creature is part of the family life. The theory of evolution does not say man is only a smarter kind of ape. It says that for two billion years living forms were tried and improved and tried and improved in preparation for the arrival of man as we know him upon the scene of life upon the earth.

And Then...Man!

A hundred years ago, all educated men

Were our ancestors apes?

were talking excitedly about the new theories of evolution. Very few of them took the trouble to read the books written by Darwin and his friends, however, and so a lot of silly ideas got started by men who thought they could get knowledge without studying. Some of these ideas were invented by people who were so sure Darwin was wicked that they made up wicked ideas and said they were Darwin's. Others were invented by people who said they were supporting Darwin, but who really meant that they wanted Darwin to support them and their own pet theories. Then the less educated people got hold of these ideas and thought that this was what the new sci-

A chimpanzee is an *anthropoid* (resembling man) ape.

though no one really knows for sure, that man and the anthropoid apes may have had a common ancestor millions of years ago, and far back along the stream of evolution. If so, it is quite certain that such a common ancestor was not an "ape," a chimpanzee or a gorilla, like the ones we see in zoos today.

Maybe the animals that were the ancestors of both apes and men — "the missing link" as some people call them

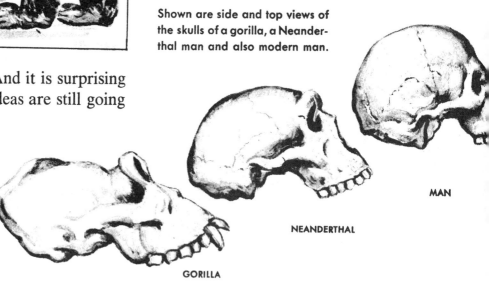

Shown are side and top views of the skulls of a gorilla, a Neanderthal man and also modern man.

MAN

NEANDERTHAL

GORILLA

ence was all about. And it is surprising how many of those ideas are still going around today.

One of these is the idea that some of the apes you can see in a zoo — the gorillas or the chimpanzees or the orangutans — are exactly like our ancestors and look like and act like they must have. Some people seem to think that one set of chimps climbed down from a tree and evolved for a million years while the rest of the chimps stayed exactly the same for a million years. This is too hard to believe.

It is somewhat easier to believe, al-

— lived so long ago that they did not look anything like apes or men. Perhaps they had not even evolved as far as monkeys. Perhaps they looked like the tarsier, a funny animal from Asia, the size of a kitten, with huge eyes. In other words, perhaps men and apes evolved side by side but quite separately from each other for many, many millions of years.

Or maybe the animals that were the ancestors of both apes and men lived

18

more recently. In that case, they probably looked somewhat more like today's apes than like today's men. In other words, since the branches of the family tree parted, the apes have been evolving more slowly than we have.

Remember, after all, that our friend in the forest in the first chapter looked a little bit apelike himself.

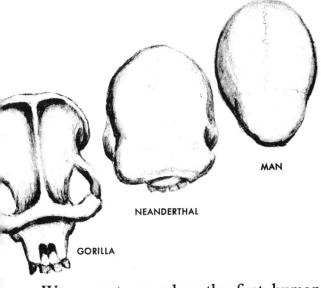

MAN

NEANDERTHAL

GORILLA

When did the first men appear? We cannot say when the first human beings appeared. There are three reasons for that. First, it is hard to say what "human" means. As far as we can tell from the bones we find, our ancestors first became "human" below the neck, and the brain followed later. But it is not walking upright, or having less body-hair, or having clumsy feet that makes us what we are. It is man's mind that makes him different from all other creatures, so we ought to say that the first true men were the first ones to have this peculiar brainpower.

Second, skeletons do not have brains. They have empty spaces where the brains used to be. We can measure these spaces. But the size of a man's head does not tell how intelligent he is. For people with small heads or big heads can be either smart or stupid. Still, since we cannot do anything else, we measure the prehistoric skulls we find and hope the numbers mean something.

Third, we have not even found enough skulls yet. What we find of these *maybe*-human creatures is often just a jawbone, or even just a tooth, and the physical anthropologists have to guess what the head was like.

All we can honestly say is this: So far we have not found anything that looks very human that is older than the beginning of the great Ice Age.

What was the Ice Age? About half a million years ago—some scientists say more and many scientists say less—the weather over the whole northern half of the earth began to change. The winters became colder. Rain and snow fell more

An iceberg breaks off from a glacier in the Ice Age.

19

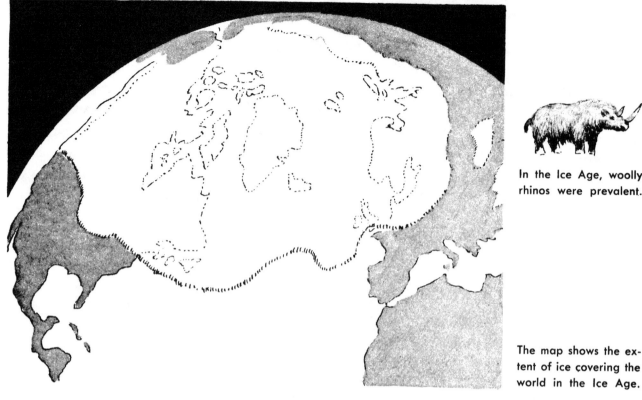

In the Ice Age, woolly rhinos were prevalent.

The map shows the extent of ice covering the world in the Ice Age.

and more of the time. In the mountainous places and up north, snow fell right through the summer. Up in the Arctic, the sheets of ice that covered land and sea grew thicker and slowly began to spread.

As wet air blew over the edge of this ice, snow kept falling and piled higher and higher, caking hard, until the edge of the great ice-sheet was a mile high. And as it inched southward, it picked up trees and great rocks. It swept the loose stones and soil before it, like a bulldozer as big as a continent. It crushed everything in its path. It pulled down mountainsides over the caves where our ancestors might have been living, and it splintered their bones in the burial grounds. Down into Europe and North America it came, grinding away the face of the earth, driving the animals before it.

This happened only in the northern hemisphere, but the amount of water there is in the world—in the seas and

rivers and lakes and in the clouds—does not change. So, as more water was frozen into the gigantic icecap, rivers and lakes dried and the level of the oceans dropped all over the globe. Islands and continents were joined together by bridges of dry land. Everywhere animals were on the move, going to live in places far from where they had evolved, and the kinds of mutations that worked well were different from the ones that worked well before.

Southward went the deer, the saber-tooth tiger, the horse. Down from the edge of the Arctic, retreating before the moving mountain of ice, came the cold-weather animals, the reindeer and the mammoth. (The last mammoths died thousands of years ago — perhaps killed off by that fierce new animal, man — yet living men have seen these great elephant-like beasts, covered with red-brown hair, as complete as if they had just died yesterday, with their last meals of grass and buttercups and fir tree branches still in their stomachs. For they were caught by the ice—falling into cracks in the glacier, or buried under avalanches—and preserved as if they had been kept in a deep-freeze. As the glacier melted, icebergs broke off and floated away northward, depositing the beasts, still frozen in huge blocks of ice and frozen mud, back in the Arctic wastelands.)

Down among the Alps in Switzerland, the ice on the mountain tops also spread, and there were times when the middle of Europe was almost cut off from the rest of the world by gigantic walls of ice. The animals caught inside this area changed—or died.

Then after thousands of years, the glaciers started to melt. Water poured down the slopes and rushed along the old river beds. The air became warmer. Inch by inch the ice retreated. The oceans and lakes began to fill again. The sun shone warmly the year round. In places where reindeer and perhaps a few manlike creatures had once shivered in the endless winter, animals from Africa now roamed. This was the "interglacial" period.

Then, thousands of years later, the glaciers came down again, and retreated, and again there was a long, sunny interglacial time when lions and hippopotamuses roamed over Europe.

Four times the ice came and four times it melted away. The last glacier retreat was only about 10,000 or 15,000 years ago. But of course . . . we do not know if it was really the last.

It was in this time of ten-thousand-year-ago summers and ten-thousand-year-ago winters that man came.

Ape-men or man-apes? In 1925, a professor in South Africa found the broken skull of a six-year-old in a layer of earth that seemed to have been formed about the same time that the glaciers were beginning at the other end of the world. The little fellow looked something like a young ape but looked human too, and the newspapers said it was "the missing link." Scientists decided it was probably a very stupid little creature, and so they called it a manlike ape.

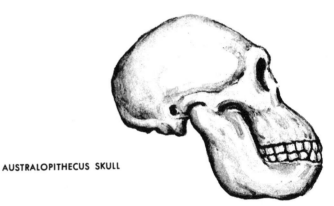

AUSTRALOPITHECUS SKULL

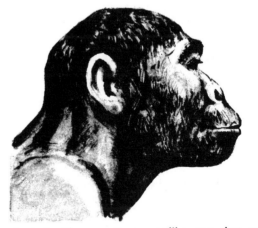

Australopithecus was a manlike ape that evolved in the south of Africa over one million years ago.

Since that discovery, many bones of grownups of the same sort have been dug up in southern Africa. Some seem to be from earlier times and some from later times. Some seem to be more man-like than others. Now no one is sure what to make of them. They have a name, though, *australopithecines* — Latin for "southern ape-like ones."

They could be just another kind of ape that happened to look more human than most and happened to die out. But not many people think so.

Or they could be our ancestors, just at the stage of evolution after they had become different from the apes' ancestors, but before they had gotten *very* different. The professors who discovered the creatures think so.

Or there might have been a time when *two* great races of intelligent beings were growing up on the planet. Perhaps the *australopithecines* had made an early start toward becoming the leaders of the family of life, but were not quite good enough. Or perhaps they had a late start and were on their way to becoming even better than men when some disaster came to them.

One thing about them is very mysterious. In several places, stone tools have been found with the bones of the *australopithecines*. Were they the creatures' own tools? Could such ape-like animals have done such human work? Or were they men's weapons? Did our ancestors, prowling the world during the Ice Age, sweep down and slaughter them?

The oldest bones that we are fairly sure

What is pithecanthropus erectus?

belong to men whose descendants are still alive were found seventy years ago on the East Indian island of

Java. The so-called Java Man had a curious career. He got his name before he was even discovered. His discoverer first decided where he ought to be and went straight there and found him — and then decided he was not very important after all. But he is very important indeed.

A hundred years ago, when Darwin's theories were being argued about, everyone agreed that if evolution was true there must have been a point when our ancestors were exactly halfway between apes and men. This is not quite so, but one scientist was so confident that he gave a name to the missing creature — *pithecanthropus erectus*, which is Latin for "ape-man who stands upright."

A young Dutch doctor named Dubois decided that the place to look for this fellow was along the banks of a certain river in the East Indies, because human remains seemed to last well there and the geologists said the river bank was about the right age. He got a job as an army surgeon and was sent to the Indies — and there, by the river, he found some teeth and the top of a skull. Then he found some leg bones. From the shape of these he brilliantly proved that this creature had a brain halfway between an ape's and a man's and walked upright. He announced that he had found the *pithecanthropus erectus*.

Of course, there was a lot of wrangling. Some people said it was an ordinary ape. Some said it was an ordinary human idiot. Dr. Dubois said firmly that it was an ape-man who walked upright — and then one day he changed

Dubois dug up the remains of *pithecanthropus erectus*.

his mind and said it was an ape after all! But by then most people agreed with his first idea.

We have now found some more of this kind of creature, and he really must have been an upright ape-man—stupid, but perhaps able to speak, and with a big flat face and almost no forehead — who lived in the South Pacific while the early part of the Ice Age was going on.

In the 1920's and 1930's, in some caves near what was called Chicken Bone Hill outside the city of Peking — now the capital of Red China — scientists dug up bits of the skulls and skeletons of about forty men, women and children.

Who was Peking Man?

They were about five feet tall and stocky. They stood straight. They seem to have been right-handed, with one side of their bodies slightly better developed than the other. Their faces were not quite as ape-like as the Java Man's, and their brains were a little bigger, but they lived about the same time as *pithecanthropus erectus* or a little later. What makes them tremendously interesting is that here at last we have found prehistoric man at home.

He was not a fellow you would care to visit for the weekend — although, surprisingly enough, he had fire and cooked some of his food, and was handy enough to make some quite useful tools by chipping and flaking pieces of stone. But either he used to have some rather unpleasant visitors or he was not fussy about his food, because the bones of wolves, wild dogs, foxes, hyenas and bears are mixed with his in the caves. There are also the bones of animals that do not live in caves, such as deer, sheep, buffaloes, bison, camels, rhinoceroses, a huge horse, ostriches and elephants. These must have been part of Peking Man's diet, for many of the bones have been split — so he could scoop out the marrow.

And there are another animal's bones on the pile — Peking Man's own bones, split for eating like the rest. He was a cannibal.

Who was the first European? Just outside the German university town of Heidelberg there is a sandpit which, for nearly a century, has been a favorite spot for geologists and paleontologists, because its neat layers show the prehistoric events of Europe very simply. In 1907, a geologist named Schoetensack found what he had been seeking for twenty years — a piece of a man. It was a jawbone, probably about 400,000 years old — perhaps as old as *pithecanthropus erectus*.

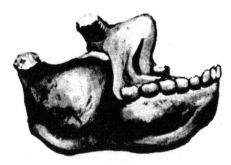

Europe's oldest trace of man: the Heidelberg jawbone.

It is the only trace of humanity found at the spot. It is the oldest trace of humanity in Europe. And it is still a mystery.

It is a jaw with all its teeth in place. The jaw is huge, chinless and rather ape-like, yet the teeth are of ordinary size and quite human.

Who was he — this flat-browed, big-headed, chinless stranger? Forty years of questioning have not brought an answer.

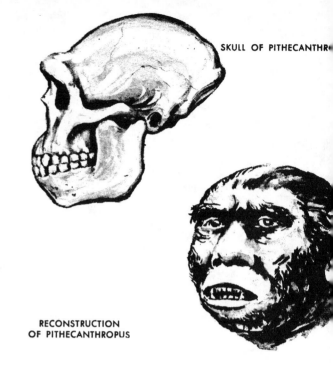

SKULL OF PITHECANTHR[...]

RECONSTRUCTION
OF PITHECANTHROPUS

Who were the Neanderthals? Before Darwin had told the world about his theories of evolution, there was already lying on a scientific society's shelves the skull of an early man — or rather an early woman — very much like what he said early humans must have been. But nobody seemed to notice it. It had been found in a cave on the Rock of Gibraltar in 1848 and given as a curiosity to the local scientific club. By the time it was sent to England, a skeleton of the same kind had been found in 1856 in a cave in the Neander Valley near the German city of Düsseldorf. So the name Neanderthal, instead of Gibraltar, was given to this kind of human being.

The Neanderthalers have been dug up in Spain, France, Belgium, Russia, Czechoslovakia, Yugoslavia and Italy. They are probably what you see in your mind's eye when you hear the words "cave man." This was a crude-faced creature with a sloping forehead, a long, wide nose, a large jaw and almost no chin. He slouched. He had big shoulders

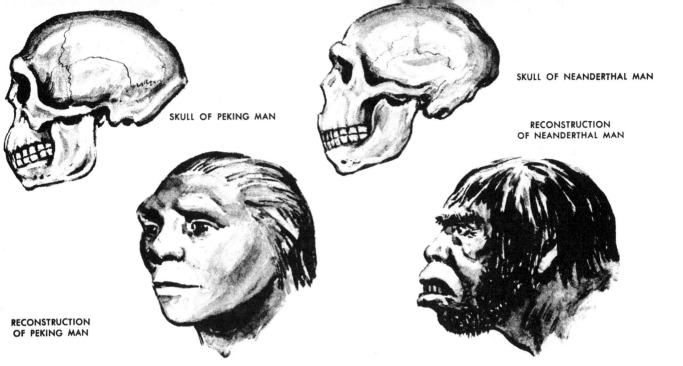

SKULL OF PEKING MAN

SKULL OF NEANDERTHAL MAN

RECONSTRUCTION
OF NEANDERTHAL MAN

RECONSTRUCTION
OF PEKING MAN

and short legs. He was a rugged fellow. He had to be. He lived in Europe in the Ice Age, 75,000 years ago. He was the man we saw in the forest in the first chapter. And by the way — he had a brain that was bigger than ours.

After Neanderthal Man was discovered, scientists soon got the idea that he was not our direct ancestor. Perhaps they hated the thought of having such a roughneck for a forefather. This fellow, they said, was another kind of man — a kind of evolutionary mistake. While Real Man, with his high forehead and fine jaw, was evolving quietly, the brawling Neanderthalers came along and bullied their way across Europe. Because they were strong, they won out during the harsh Ice Age. Because they were stupid, they lost in the end.

It was a good story. It seemed quite a clever way to explain the strange fact that there were some men from *before* Neanderthal times who in some ways looked less like apes and more like us.

But in 1931 and 1932, some American and English scientists found two adjoining caves on Mount Carmel in Palestine — now Israel — which contained the remains of a dozen people, along with their stone tools. The bones from one cave—Mugharet es Skhul, the Cave of the Young Goats—were a mixture of Modern and Neanderthal, mostly Modern, while some of the bones from next door were very Neanderthal. The more the scientists studied these finds, the more it seemed that Moderns and Neanderthalers had married each other and had children who had children. This was a very startling idea. Because the geneticists say definitely that this could not have happened if the Neanderthals were really on a different evolutionary path.

So the picture we now have of our Ice Age ancestors is this: Most scientists think that up to 150,000 years ago or so, there was one and only one basic kind of man. He was spread out over Europe, Asia, the South Pacific and Africa. Of course, there are some pretty noticeable differences between the people in those places — just as there are

25

today. We can easily tell the difference between, say, the peoples of Scandinavia, the Soviet Union, the Mideast, the Far East, Africa, and Latin America. Many characteristics will often identify an ethnic or national background.

Then the terrible cold of the last glacier began to close in on Europe. A lot of the various tribes got out, going to places like Palestine. But a few were caught in Western Europe, surrounded by water and ice and freezing open plains. These diehard Europeans developed a special rugged build and appearance which was just an exaggeration of what they had started with — they were the Neanderthalers. When the glacier moved back a little, and they were finally able to reach the rest of the world, they mixed with the rest of mankind.

Sometimes they mixed a little more thoroughly with other people than they probably wanted to — some workers in a stone-quarry, in the section of south-western Europe which is now called Yugoslavia, discovered some Neanderthal bones neatly split for eating. But just as often, no doubt, the Neanderthalers married with the other peoples, and soon lost their identity.

Here and there in Europe, perhaps as early as the middle of the Ice Age, there were a few breeds of men who looked much more modern than the tough Neanderthalers. A girl of twenty was found in some gravel near the Thames River in England. She was in a layer that contained the bones of rhinoceroses and elephants, which were

Who were the first "modern" men?

supposed to have come up from Africa and roamed in England during the long warm spell between the second and third glaciers. Yet this very old young lady is practically like an English girl of today.

A cave at Fontéchevade in France has yielded skulls similar to those of modern Frenchmen. Yet they were in with the bones of certain types of deer, tortoises and rhinoceroses that are supposed to belong to the warm period between the third and fourth glaciers.

As the Ice Age drew near its end, many interesting new types of people seem to have moved into what had been Neanderthal territory. The most famous is the Old Man of Cro-Magnon, found with four other skeletons in the Cro-Magnon cave in south central France. This man is typical of one of the two main kinds of people who were cropping up everywhere 15,000 years ago. He is a

little over five feet six inches tall, and he has a splendid big head — it held about ten percent more brains than the average European has today — with a high forehead and a good strong chin. The Cro-Magnon people looked a lot like modern Swedes and Norwegians.

The other main type of Late Ice Age people is called the Combe-Capelle type, also discovered in south central France. These were shorter folk than the Cro-Magnons, and they had big eye-brow-ridges and jaws — though not nearly as big as the Neanderthalers' — but their foreheads and chins were almost similar to our own.

Up to a few years ago, many people believed that we descended from the Cro-Magnons and only from the Cro-Magnons. They believed this mainly because they wanted to — the Cro-Magnons were the best-looking of all prehistoric men. Now we know that the

Combe-Capelle and many other people were also mixed up in our ancestry.

At this point in our story we have, in fact, come so close to home that it is infuriating not to know more about all these people and what became of them. Europe and Asia and the Near East (that vital spot where so much of human history has started) were soon to be the scene of huge battles and far wanderings, of brilliant inventions and ignorant destructions, of mass disappearances and silent arrivals.

Did these cave-dwellers set out during the great thaw of 15,000 years ago and carry the sound of the human voice and the smoke of the campfire and the deadly cleverness of human fingers into the ancient wilderness? Did they meet older and simpler peoples on the way and slaughter the men and drag the frightened women and children along on their endless march? Did they become the fathers of new breeds of men, mixing the designs stored in their twists of nucleic acid with the mutations from hundreds of distant caves and rock-shelters?

Or did they stay in Europe? Or did some other breed of men, from some corner of the world which we have not explored, break in upon them and hunt them from valley to valley, as the white men broke in on the American Indians and hunted them, until only a handful were left in out-of-the-way forests?

Down on the French Riviera is the little principality of Monaco, famous for its gambling casino and its lovely Amer-

Were the early Europeans white men?

The cave-dwelling Cro-Magnons had to kill or drive away uninvited guests.

27

ican princess. Here, sixty years ago, in a cave called the Grotto of the Children, were found the bones of the lady known to anthropologists as the Widow of Grimaldi, along with her teenage son. They are a little like the Cro-Magnons, but there are some interesting things about them. No one, of course, can tell from a man's bones what color his skin was. But many physical anthropologists are convinced from the shape of the face and the length of the shins and forearms that here, on the north coast of the Mediterranean Sea, we have found two of the ancestors of the modern Negroes of Africa. Some even think they come from the time when the Africans were beginning to develop into a special kind of people.

And, once again in south central France, we have the famous Chancelade skeleton — the bones of a short, sturdy man of about sixty. He looks very much like an Eskimo, and a few scientists actually think he was an ancestor of the Eskimos, but even though we know nothing about the Eskimos until they suddenly appear about 2000 B.C., this is rather hard to believe. A famous anthropologist named Hooton said Chancelade man might have looked that way because his food was tough, like the tough fish that develops the Eskimo's jaws. Whoever these strangers were, it certainly was at this time that the hunters, forming themselves into bands and prowling the world for meat, began to divide into the races we know today.

The word "race" is a deadly word. A **What is a race?** few decades ago, six million Jewish people were murdered at the orders of the madman Hitler because he thought he belonged to a "master race" and his helpless victims belonged to a "lower race." The word "race" is dangerous because it is used with many different meanings, and most of them are cruel nonsense.

To the scientist — to the geneticist and the anthropologist — there is only one proper meaning: A race is a group of people who have had the same ancestors in recent times and whose bodies look pretty much alike. By bodies the scientists mean people's skin, hair, eyes, teeth, bones, blood cells and things like that — but not people's minds.

Scientists have studied people's minds very carefully. The nucleic acids that contain the master plan of a human being will sometimes decide whether he has a clever brain or a stupid brain, but they have nothing to say about what ideas there will be in that brain. Suppose we took an Eskimo baby to the South Sea Islands and raised him as a South Sea Islander. He would grow up looking like an Eskimo — short, with a wide, flat face, eyes with the slanting fold of skin over the corners, and straight black hair — not like a tall, brown-haired Tahitian. But he would think like a Tahitian. He would love the big round fruit of the breadfruit tree, while seal blubber would make him feel sick to his stomach. He would think that a loincloth made of pounded tree-bark was the only proper thing for a man to wear, and if we showed him a picture of his own father dressed in a fur parka, he would wonder who this strange, primitive creature could be.

There are as many different types of

Why did races evolve?

human bodies as there are kinds of places where humans live. The differences are astonishing. There are the almost blue-black Papuans of the South Pacific and the pale pink Northern Europeans. There are the fat Eskimos in Greenland and the skinny Bushmen of the Kalahari Desert in southern Africa. There are the Watusi Negroes of Africa, seven feet tall, and the Pygmies of Africa, four feet tall. And all go back to the same prehistoric ancestors.

While we still do not know very much about why such differences came about, we have discovered several fascinating facts. They all point to the same thing: All these race differences are ways in which men have become *specialists* in living in certain kinds of places.

Take skin color, for instance. There are

Why are some races dark-skinned?

three kinds of skin: a pinkish - white kind, which gets badly "burned" rather than "tanned" by sunlight; a chocolate-brown or black kind, which is not hurt by the fiercest sunlight; and a change-able kind — it may look white or olive or reddish or brownish — which turns tanner or paler according to how much sunlight touches it, and this last is the kind of skin which most of mankind has.

Sunlight contains ultra-violet rays

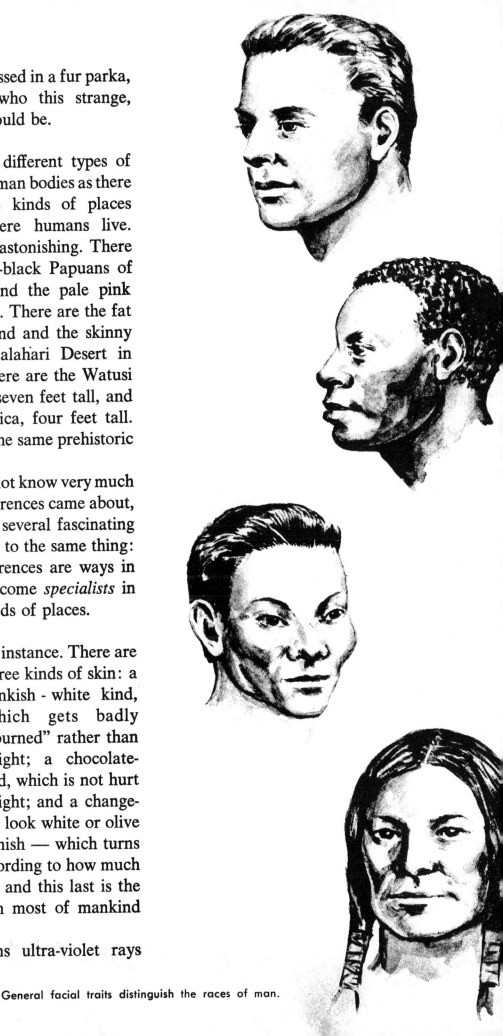

General facial traits distinguish the races of man.

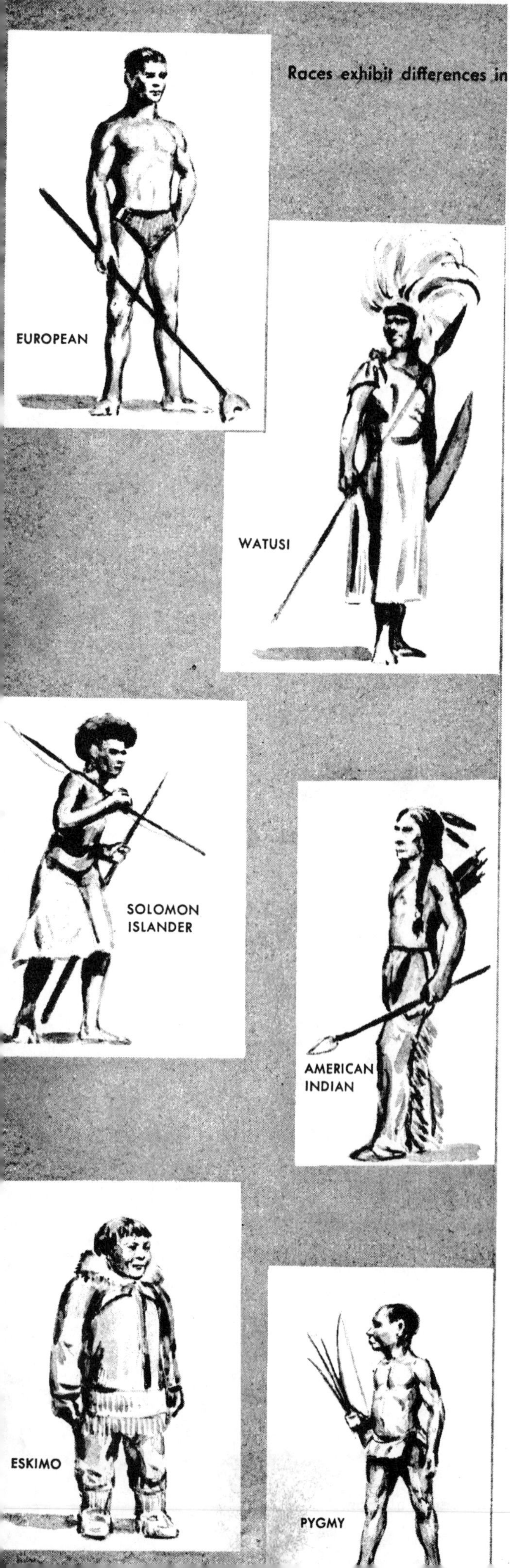

Races exhibit differences in stature and body build.

EUROPEAN

WATUSI

SOLOMON
ISLANDER

AMERICAN
INDIAN

ESKIMO

PYGMY

which are both good and bad for people. When they "irradiate" certain fats just beneath the skin, they produce Vitamin D, which is important for our bones. But too much sunlight can cause damage — painful sores and sunstroke.

The body chemical that colors the skin tan or brown has a way of absorbing and stopping ultra-violet rays.

In places like northwestern Europe, where the sunlight is weak and there is a lot of cloudy weather, people with the pinkish-white skin that does not have this chemical are better off than others, because their bodies can make more Vitamin D. And that is exactly where most of the pinkish-white people are found.

In places like the grasslands of Africa near the equator, the sunlight beats down mercilessly, and it is too hot to wear much clothing. A hunter who must get his food under that blazing sky is much better off if his skin is filled with the protective coloring-matter. And it is just in those places that the darkest-skinned people of the world are found.

Many physical anthropologists believe that man as he originally evolved had the changeable kind of skin that most men still have, which gets lighter in the winter and darker in the summer. But there were always some children born with mutations that caused permanently light skin and some born with mutations that caused permanently dark skin. Among the prehistoric Europeans who lived near the glacier, where the sky was always filled with snow-clouds, the light-skin mutation won out. Down in the equatorial plains, the black-skin mutation won.

The natural shape of a soap bubble is round. That is because a sphere is the shape, which, as the mathematicians say, "has the least surface for a given volume." In other words, there is a certain amount of air in the bubble, and the soapy skin has to go around the outside of it, but since the skin is always trying to shrink, the air gets squeezed into the shape that needs the smallest outside skin or surface. A long, thin, cigar-shaped bubble would take much more soap-skin to hold the same amount of air. And *that* is why the Eskimos, for instance, look the way they do.

Why are some races pudgy?

The Eskimos live in the icy north, on the edge of what is left of the Ice Age glacier. Many of them live in igloos, huts built out of blocks of ice. Even though they are wrapped in furs, they are never really warm. So their race has specialized in cold-weather living.

They are very round people, so they have room in their bodies for plenty of fat, which helps to hold in the body-heat and also helps them to live through the terrible weeks when seal or fish are scarce; and at the same time they do not have so much skin-surface to be cooled by the freezing air.

Their faces work the same way. Some physical anthropologists say that if you were to sit down and redesign your own face to protect it against the cold, you would end up with an Eskimo face. The slanting folds of skin around the eyes protect them from frosty air as well as from blinding reflections off the white snow. The flat brows and fat cheeks protect the delicate sinuses from cold. The wide, big cheek bones shield both eyes and nose. Above all, the flat face keeps most of the features close to its round surface, instead of having them stick out where they can get frostbitten.

The Eskimos have stubby legs and arms. The Watusi Negroes of Africa, the tallest men on earth, have the longest and lankiest legs and arms. For their problem is the opposite of the Eskimos — they have to have a lot of skin surface to keep their bodies cool. You have noticed, of course, that when you wet your skin, even with warm water, it quickly begins to feel cool; evaporation cools. And this is why you sweat when you are overheated — it is your body's emergency cooling system. Now, a long, thin shape has a great deal of surface considering the amount of material inside; and if a man's legs and arms are lanky, his sweat-cooled skin can do the most efficient work in drawing off the heat from his blood-vessels, and thus cool the whole body.

A scientist, like any other man, is proud of his own kind of people. But he is more proud of being honest. And so scientists who have studied other races of men — they are called *ethnologists,* which is Greek for "talkers about nations" — have usually reported that no matter where you go in the world and no matter what the people look like, there are some stupid ones and some clever ones and most are about the same.

Are some races smarter?

This is probably because good brains help a man stay alive in any part of the world, so no group has evolved much

31

The Yahgan Indians of Tierra del Fuego discovered by Captain Cook in 1774 did not develop beyond a primitive existence. Yet more than 2,000 years earlier in Guatemala and Yucatán, the Mayan Indians already had a flourishing civilization. Above: a Yahgan hut; left and below a Mayan palace, Yucatan ornaments

faster or further than others, at least above the neck. Here and there, a band of prehistoric men may have wandered into some desolate part of the world where there is not much a man can do to make himself safer or healthier. For example, the natives of Tierra del Fuego at the southernmost tip of South America might well have been less smart than the other Indians to the north, even though they must have come from the same ancestors. And this could have been because the climate was so cold and harsh, and the things a man could use to make his life easier were so scarce, that the people who stayed alive the longest were the dull ones who could stand discomfort.

Always remember this: Men are men. There are no men now alive who are "nearer to the apes" than others.

Man's Works

The town of Abbeville lies near the northern coast of France, where the River Somme flows out into the English Channel. In the year 1830, Jacques Boucher de Crévecoeur de Perthes held the job of customs official in the town. He was supposed to inspect the cargoes of all the ships that sailed into the river mouth and make sure that the taxes were paid. It was not a hard job, so Boucher de Perthes had time to read about geology and to write stories and plays and books on government problems.

What were the first traces of early man?

One day, as he was taking his afternoon walk along the road that followed the river bank, he came upon some workmen. He stood watching them, the skirts of his greatcoat flapping in the damp sea breeze. Suddenly his eye caught a strangely shaped stone in the gravel river bank where they were digging. He walked over and picked it up. And modern man discovered his prehistoric ancestors.

It was a flint pebble shaped like a pear, and the narrower end had been chipped away to form a jagged point. The chipping could not have been accidental. A man must have done it.

Boucher de Perthes looked down at the layers of packed-down gravel, hundreds and hundreds of centuries old, where the stone had been buried, and asked himself: "But what man *could* have done this?" For in those days no one thought man had been on the earth for more than 6,000 years. He shifted the stone in his hand so that the round end nestled in his palm, and in his mind's eye he saw not his own smooth white fingers holding an interesting pebble, but the hairy fist of some man of incredibly ancient times clutching a sharp stone claw as he chopped at a savage enemy.

But although Boucher de Perthes had the imaginative mind of a writer of stories when he looked at the fist-axe, he also had the cautious mind of a government official. He said nothing. He came to the river road during his spare time and dug in the gravel. Where the flint tool had been lying, he found the bones of elephants and rhinoceroses! A great new story of prehistoric Europe formed in his mind, but still he said nothing.

It was not until sixteen years later that he sat down to write his book proving that there had been men on earth — tool-using men — fifty or a hundred thousand years before. And it was fifteen years more before the last scoffing professor was convinced. And by that

Abbevillian bifaces: one of man's early stone tools.

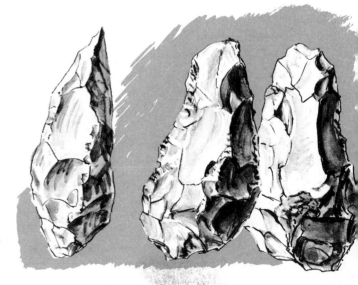

time Darwin had written his great book and the skulls of prehistoric men had been found.

Stand in front of the mirror. Look. You **What is a tool?** are a wonderfully designed animal. You are standing on your hind legs, and that means that your front limbs are free to fight or to point or to lift things. They do not have to help you move around, as a horse's or a tiger's do.

Lift your arm. Look. This forelimb of yours is a powerful instrument. It has a ball-and-socket joint at the shoulder. It has a strong folding joint at the elbow. It has a turning joint at the wrist. It has a very clever system of muscle-cables inside its skin to control this useful apparatus. You can move heavy things easily.

Hold out your hand. Look. Each of your fingers bends in three places. You can turn your thumb so that it lies right across the palm of your hand. You can grip big things and little things. You can hold them tightly or firmly. You can twist, turn, pull, push or throw things of any shape. Backing up the tips of your fingers are the tough flat nails. They make the ends of your fingers stiff enough to hold things without your having skin so coarse and hard that you could not do delicate work. Your hand is a tool that makes it possible for you to have other tools.

Yet other animals are almost as well designed as you are. Apes can walk on their hind legs, though they normally get a little help from their hands. They can cross their thumbs over, and they can hold and move things in their

AXE

HARPOON

fingers. But they do not use tools. Their brains lack something.

When your hairy ancestor picked up a sharp stone to scrape something or a heavy stone to hammer something, it was a tremendous idea. *He was making an addition to his body. His mind was giving his body a new power over the world around him.*

And when he could not find the right stone, and instead of poking in the gravel all day for what he wanted, he just picked up another stone and chipped the first stone into the right shape, it was an even more tremendous idea. *He was changing the world around him to fit himself. His mind gave him a picture of something good that did not exist yet and he made it exist.*

The ordinary animal needs certain things — certain foods, certain shelter, a certain climate. When the things

HAND AXE

Where workmen were dredging a river bank, Boucher de Perthes dug up animal bones and tools of early man.

SOUTH AFRICAN PEBBLE TOOL

AWL

around him are not what he needs, he goes somewhere else. Birds and bees build nests. Spiders make webs. Beavers build dams. But if they do not have the right tree or corner or stream, they cannot design a new kind of nest or web or dam, and they cannot change the tree or corner or stream that is there. They have to go away.

But when a man first changed the shape of a stone, he became the first animal that said: "World, we don't suit each other, you and I — and *you're* going to change!"

And from that moment on, man was surely going to have weapons, which were killing-tools.

And fire, which changed food and climate for him.

And clothing, which was portable shelter.

And art, which was a way his mind

SPEARHEAD

told itself about the things he wanted, but did not have yet.

And language, which started as a way of pointing at things and became a way his mind told other minds about things that were not around for him to point at.

And, much later, herds of animals and fields full of crops, which were man's way of saying to all other living things: "I chose *you* to live in this world with me and for me, and *you others* I don't want."

If one of our man-ape ancestors needed

What were the first tools? a heavy stone to hammer something or a sharp stone to scrape something, he poked around until he found one, and when he finished with it he would throw it away. He had no pockets, because he had no clothes.

And when the ape-man changed the shape of a stone to make it more useful, he naturally chose the stone that needed the least work done on it. And the work he did on it by chipping or splitting was so crude that we usually cannot tell it from accidental chipping or splitting.

Museums are full of what are called *eoliths* — Greek for "dawn stones" — which are supposed to be these earliest work tools. But it is hard to see the human workmanship in most of them.

MORTAR

The earliest tools we have found that

How old are the earliest tools? show pretty definite signs of having been worked on by men seem to be older than any of the men we have found. They have

PIERCER

NEEDLES

been dug up in Africa, both in the south and in the north of that mysterious continent. Some of them are more than a half-million years old.

They are split pebbles larger than your fist, with one side chipped to make a sort of sharp edge. As the first glacier sent the ape-men roaming over the wildernesses of the Old World between the Ice and the fiery desert, these "pebble tools" must have spread from one wandering band to another.

Then, over thousands and thousands of years, the bands in the west — in Europe and Africa and Central Asia — began to improve their crude implements. The bands of the east — in what is now China and the South Sea Islands — learned to improve theirs, too, but in a different way.

Stone Age man chipped pieces from a chunk of flint to make a fist-axe.

Nobody knows when primitive man succeeded in making fire, but it was a giant step.

How were "fist-axes" made? Around the time of the second glacier, perhaps 300,000 to 400,000 years ago, word spread among the western peoples of an important invention. It was the "fist-axe" — though probably the tool was used for prying and picking and scraping as much as for chopping. The technical name for it is "core-biface," because when prehistoric man made it by chipping away at a pear-shaped stone to form an edge or point, he kept the big stone or "core" and threw the chips away — and he chipped at both sides or "faces" of it.

This was the tool that Boucher de Perthes found in the gravel of the Somme River. Many like it have been found all over Africa, Europe and Central Asia. Who used them? We do not know. We have never found them together with their owners — at least, not until we come to the handsome core-bifaces that were still being made hundreds of thousands of years later.

One day, while the western tribes were still just learning how to make core-bifaces, a great scientific genius was sitting on a gravel heap making himself a large fist-axe. He struck too hard with his hammer-

How are "flake tools" made?

37

stone, and instead of the neat little chip he wanted to take off, a wide, flat flake fell to the ground. He picked it up and looked at it. He felt its sharp edge and his eyes under the heavy brow-ridges narrowed. He was thinking about stones in a new way. He tried to remember how he had held the core-stone and the hammer-stone, and he struck again. An ordinary chip fell off. Again. A fair-sized flake. Again. A beautiful thin, sharp tool.

Soon the news was passed from tribe to tribe that if you could find good core-stones you could make many handfuls of tools from one stone, and make them quickly.

It used to be thought that the people who made core-bifaces and the people who made flake tools were different kinds of men. Some scientists even had visions of great wars fought all over the west between core-bifaces and flakers, and a few even dreamed of Neanderthal villains with jagged little flakes fighting Cro-Magnon heroes carrying well-made core-bifaces. Others argued that the same men probably had both kinds of tools. After all, we have many kinds of tools and we do not have wars between Wrench Tribes, Pliers Tribes, Razor Tribes and Screwdriver Tribes. In 1906, a Frenchman digging near the Somme River — the same river where prehistoric tools were first found — came upon a gravel pit which had been used as an open-air workshop. And here some very early men had worked side by side making core-bifaces and flake-tools.

For untold centuries, these two kinds of stones were the tool-kit and armory of the west.

Of all the early stone tools, the only ones that have been found along with their owners are the tools with Peking Man at Chicken Bone Mountain. They are also the only early ones found in a cave. The rest were all found out in the open.

What tools did Peking Man use?

These eastern tools are quite different from the tools used in Europe. They are what are called "chopper-chopping tools." Some are wide scrapers. Some are heavy cleavers. Some have points. But big or small, wide or pointed, they are made like "hand adzes." An adze is a little different from an axe. The cutting edge of an axe is sharpened on both faces; the edge of an adze is chipped away on one face only. No doubt they were useful in splitting bones during feasts.

An ax is shaped like this:

An adze is shaped like this.

For two or three thousand centuries, while the ice closed in and drew back again and again, man produced no really new ideas. The old ways of mak-

What did man invent in the Ice Age?

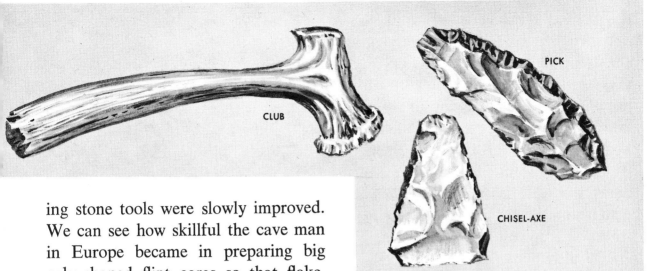

CLUB

PICK

CHISEL-AXE

ing stone tools were slowly improved. We can see how skillful the cave man in Europe became in preparing big cake-shaped flint cores so that flake-tool after flake-tool could be whacked off with swift, clean blows. The core-bifaces begin to be flat and even-shaped and sharp.

Then, in the warm spell before the last glacier, there was a great stirring among the minds of the prehistoric men of Europe. By the time the mountains of ice came grinding down, men had set up tribe-households in caves. They began to make tools out of new materials, and their stone tools took new forms. During the endless winter, they invented throwing-sticks to help their arms hurl their spears farther. They tied strips of animal hide together to make ropes, and attached bone har-

poons to them with cleverly carved barbs to catch in the flesh of animals. They made bows and arrows, and some of their arrows had bone tips. Their stone spear-points and arrowheads were as fine as laurel leaves. They learned to use long cone-shaped flint cores from which they could flake off knife-blades and chisels. As the Ice Age came to an end, the men who followed the glaciers up from the Mediterranean Sea were making very small, delicately-worked stone arrowheads and tools which we call *microliths* (Greek for "tiny stones").

Story of the Cave Man Paintings

He was afraid. He squatted in the yellow dancing firelight next to the other young men of the cave, and he hoped they would not see how his lips and his fingers were shaking. For the time had again come when he must go

down into The Darkness, down into the hungry belly of the earth.

For many days now — ever since this moon was born — the hunting had been bad, and the people of the cave were weak from lack of food. Yesterday an old woman and a young girl had died. The cunning old hunters and the strong young hunters went out early every day, and came back late — with nothing but their dry, clean spears and knives. All the berries and nuts had long ago been stripped from the branches. There were two children who were already too weak to walk, and an old man who once was wise and merry but who now slept all day and all night.

The men of the cave met together and decided. Some said this moon was a Moon of Weakness, and the hunters would have no power over the animals until the moon grew fat and thin and died, and a new, thin sliver of moon was born in the sky. But others said that the Magic of the cave was all used up, and more Magic must be made. Then the first ones said that Magic could do nothing under a Moon of Weakness, and the new Magic must be made at the birth of

Led by a chanting Healer, the cave men danced as a means of attaining power over animals they hunted.

Cave man artists sought power over the animals which they depicted in color on the cave walls.

the new moon. But the others said that the people of the cave could not wait, for the new moon would not be born for two-handfuls-and-three-more-fingers of days. And so the decision was that the Healer would dance tonight and the chosen men — an old man and a young man — would go down into the belly of the earth, away from the sight of the

Moon of Weakness, and make the Magic of Power.

And he was the chosen young man. He licked his dry lips.

Next to him, his younger brother was preparing for tomorrow's great hunt. He was making a new spear-thrower. He had taken one of the great antlers he and his father had saved from many hunts, and had broken off all the points until he had a fine straight piece of horn. Now he was smoothing it with a beautiful flint blade their father had just made. Carefully the boy formed it, a thin rod as long as his forearm, with a little groove and a notch that turned the end of it into a hook. Throwers were hard to use — you held the thrower with three fingers of your hand, the hook pointed back past your shoulder. You laid the spear along the thrower, with the blunt end nestling back against the hook and the spearhead forward, while you held the middle of the spear-shaft with the other two fingers of your throwing hand. Then a swift, whipping throw — with the extra reach that the thrower gave your arm — and the spear whistled forward faster than any man's arm alone could have hurled it. It was hard, but young as little brother was, he was making a good thrower, and he could use it well.

Their father was making spear points. The old man had the Rain Sickness in his fingers, and the swollen knuckles did not bend well any more. Yet the wisdom of many years was still in his hands, and he could make the terrible weapons he could not use. He had a large chunk of flint that he had carefully chipped down into a cone shape — this was the Mother of Blades. Against it he held the tip of a little punch made of bone, and whacked it with the hammer-stone, the Father of Blades. And so keen was the old man's eye and so great was the cunning of his hands that each whack chipped off a flat blade with the lovely, deadly-sharp edges that only good flint could give.

Whack! Whack! Whack! Three perfect blades. They would make good knives to cut meat. With a little chipping, they would make scrapers to clean the animal hides, or punches to sew the hides into clothing. But tonight the people had no meat and no furs — they still had to get them. So the old man began to chip at the beautiful blades, taking off tiny flakes until he had fashioned a spearhead shaped like

Early man scraped the tough, rough hides of animals with stone implements to soften the skins which clothed him.

a leaf, a leaf of death, a leaf of power.

The young man looked from his busy brother to his busy father, and then looked down at the strange tools beside his own feet: The little bone pot, made of rabbit's skull, filled with black soot from the fire; the stone pots with lumps of sun-dried red clay and yellow clay in them; the little strip of hide; the skull-bowls of water; and the unlit lamps composed of three shallow stone basins, with wicks made of the braided hair of young girls, filled with the last animal fat that the people of the cave had. (There had been five lamps, but a hungry child had drunk the fat from two of them.) These were his tools, the tools of the Magic of Power.

Slowly and with unsteady hands, he began to crush the colored clay into powder, using a round pebble. The powder must be fine, must be perfect. He was so absorbed in his task that he did not notice when the sounds of the stone-chipping and wood-scraping died down and the talking stopped and a hush fell over the people of the cave. But he heard the hoarse voice of the Healer say, "Come!" and he stood up. The older chosen man helped him to pour and mix the water into the pots of black, red and yellow powder, and to light two of the lamps at the fire. He carried one lighted lamp and the black pot. The Healer carried the other lighted lamp and the old red pot. The young man carried the unlit lamp and the yellow pot, along with the strips of hide. They turned from the fire, which was at the cave entrance, and walked into the darkness at the back of the cave.

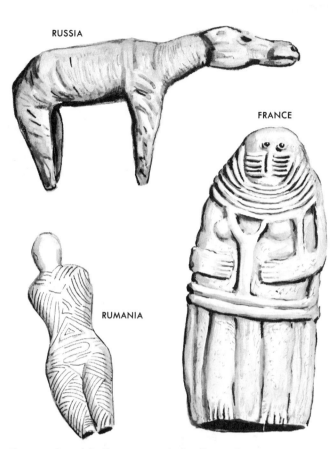

RUSSIA

FRANCE

RUMANIA

Figures, found in Europe, made by Stone Age men.

The men of the cave followed a little way behind, their hands full of spears and spear-throwers and stone knives. The silent procession passed into the deepest shadows, and stooped, one by one, to go into the small black hole in the wall of the cave.

The sputtering lamps cast a faint, shaky glow on the sides of the narrow passage. It was cold, but it was not the cold that made the young man's teeth chatter as he followed the Healer and the old man.

Behind him, there were groans and mumblings of fright from some of the men, and fierce whispers to be quiet from others. Was there a snake's hiss?

Down they went, into the dim vault of another cavern, where the two crackling braids of hair in the bowls of ani-

One of the most beautiful examples of early cave man paintings was found in southwestern France at Lascaux Cave.

A cave wall frequently shows stenciled hands, sometimes even mutilated as the cave man's hand might have been.

mal fat showed the bones of a bear and several smaller animals. A rat scurried almost under their feet and ran squeaking into the darkness. They came to another passage-entrance, and suddenly one of the men threw down his weapons and began to run the way they had come. "Come back!" someone cried, and the whole group called, "Come back! Come back!" But it was not necessary. The frightened man took ten steps into the awful shadows, stopped, turned, and ran back to catch up with the disappearing glow of the two lamps. Others had picked up his weapons before the light was gone.

At last they came to the place. The men piled their weapons in the center of the dark cave, calling each by name. Their eyeballs gleamed yellow in the lamplight as they looked toward the Healer. From among the spears, he drew a noble pair of deer antlers attached to a strip of deerhide and quickly tied them to his head.

He began his chant, calling the animals of the forest by their Own Names, and boasting loudly of the Power of the people of the cave and the Power of the weapons over all animals.

Meanwhile, some of the hunters ran to the wall of the cavern and held their right hands flat against it. The old chosen man and the young chosen man hastily dipped the strips of fur into the paint-bowls and traced the outlines of the hands on the stone, some in red, some in black, some in yellow. There were great, strong, young hands. There were old hands knotted with the Rain Sickness. There were hands with two or even three fingers missing. Swiftly they were painted on the wall, and then the hunters gathered near the old man who, holding one lamp aloft, led them into the passages through which they had come.

They stumbled in their hurry, for there was not much grease left in their lamp-bowl, and if the flame died out before they reached the outer cave, they might wander in the blackness into a wrong passage and be lost, swallowed in the earth's belly.

The young man and the Healer were left alone.

The Healer danced, calling more and more wildly on the animals to submit to the Power of man. Name after name he shouted, names of animals, names of the winds, names of weapons, the secret words of Power.

And the young man painted. First he drew a great bison, proud in its huge strength, with the rich folds of fat and muscle hanging down between its thin, short forelegs, and the tail lashing. A rub of black and a rub of yellow, quickly made with the little fur strips — and the brown of the big beast's fur was properly caught on the cave wall. The small red-rimmed eyes with the staring black dots in the center — and the animal's fierce temper was caught.

"Submit! Submit!" chanted the Healer, calling the bison by name. "The Power is man's!"

The young man forgot to tremble with fear. He forgot to hurry. He forgot to watch the sputtering lamp on the floor by his feet, to see when it was burning low and the other lamp must be lighted. He was painting the proudest and strongest of all bisons, catching its living strength and its terrible spirit on the wall of the cave.

It was the Healer who stopped his chant and, just in time, leaped to the lamp as the flame started to sink and grow dim. If the new lamp was not lighted from the old, they would be lost forever. Feverishly, he held the hair-wick of the unlighted lamp to the dying flame. It caught, smoked, and went out, caught again, smoked, and went out. "Power of Fire! Power of Fire!" shrieked the Healer, and called the secret name of the Sun Itself. Just as the old lamp died, the tiny flame of the new one hung for a moment on a bubble of the fat, smoked dangerously, and then started to grow bright.

The Healer drew off his deerskin breech-clout and his tiger-skin cape and began to pile the weapons in them, throwing the used-up lamp onto one pile and tying it up in a bundle. "Come! Come now!" he said harshly.

But the young man had more work to do. He had begun to paint a deer. "Dance!" he said in a low voice. "Sing, dance! The people are dying of hunger. The Magic must be strong!" His hand, holding the soot-black fur, swept over the wall and traced the strong line of the animal's flanks as it leaped in the air. His fingers dipped another fur-strip in the red pot and began the coloring and shading of the muscles in the neck and legs. There was an old, dried painting of a mammoth in the way, left by some earlier people of the cave. The young man painted over it as if it were not there.

The Healer's chant was quick and all the wildness had gone out of it, and soon he called, "Come! Do you hear!"

The young man flung the empty paint pots into the second pile of weapons, tied it all up in the fur cape, and staggered as he lifted the huge bundle. He also slung the other bundle over his shoulder, held the lamp high, and led the way up through the darkness toward the campfire and the people waiting for the dawn and the hunt.

How Did Civilization Come to the Cave Men?

About 15,000 years ago, the last glacier (we hope) began its last retreat from Europe. By 10,000 B.C., the big hardy animals that lived at the edge of the cold — the mammoth and the woolly rhinoceros—had crashed away through the northern forests and were dying out. The reindeer were moving north. The forests were full of smaller, swifter animals. The seasons were different. The rising oceans poured into the lowlands, and England and Ireland turned into islands. The Forest People came out of their caves and built summer camps by the shores of lakes. They tamed the dog, but they did not know what a tremendous idea was wagging its tail at their very feet. They even forgot their beautiful art. As change followed change, they had to turn their minds to ingenious new hunting-weapons of wood and bone, and new tools, and new kinds of camps.

We have found a camp of the Forest People, wonderfully preserved in a great swamp in Denmark. It is the home of clever, practical people, but not people with great new ideas, not people who were inventing civilization. Europe, where man had done so much and learned so much, was now just an out-of-the-way place.

In the Middle East, in what is now the Arab country of Iraq, flowed two mighty rivers, the Tigris and the Euphrates, bringing water and life in a great green streak across the harsh plains and hills. The streak bent over westward to the Syrian shore of the Mediterranean Sea, and southward to where the Biblical city of Jericho was later to stand. It was in this Fertile Crescent, as we now call it, that human civilization began ten thousand years ago.

Where did civilization begin?

On the slopes above the two rivers grew certain wild plants — wheat and barley. Certain wild animals — goats, pigs, sheep, horses, oxen and dogs — roamed the lower hills. Perhaps it was a hunter running with his dog who said: "If I can tame a dog — why not a goat, a horse, a sheep?" Or perhaps it was a mother, gathering the little kernels of wheat, who said: "Why, these are the seeds of the wheat plant! If I put them in the ground next to my shelter, the plant will grow there and I will not have to walk so far."

Anyway, the enormous idea came into the minds of men. They became food *producers* instead of food *gatherers*. By 9000 B.C., they were planting and harvesting crops.

A man who goes from cave to cave or hut to hut, following the animals he

From a cave to the lake-dweller's hut was a big step.

Man became a food *producer* instead of a *gatherer*.

eats, does not build a good hut or home — he has no time, and anyway he will not use it for long. He has no breakable possessions and very little clothing, because he must always be ready to carry everything he owns.

But a man who grows crops and tends flocks knows he will stay in one place. He builds a good house and a barn or silo to store his grain. He gives his family work to do. He lives close to his neighbors so everyone can help with the planting and harvesting and the guarding of the sheep. He builds a village. By 8000 B.C. there were many villages.

There were water-springs in the hills above the slopes of the Fertile Crescent. Sometimes the two rivers raged out of control and carried away the homes and flocks and crops of the farmers. If the farmers could build earth walls, the waters could be sent only into fields that needed it, and if the farmers could dig ditches to let the water flow from the springs down to the dry fields, they could plant crops back away from the river, where they would be safer. So irrigation was invented before 4000 B.C.

Men learned to mold clay into bowls and bake it. The bowls would have been too breakable for hunter families, but they were needed by farm families. Pottery had been invented by 5000 B.C.

The village grew into cities. Men exchanged their goods and traded. Money was invented. And the news of these great ideas traveled into Europe. By 3000 B.C., farming had spread to France and Spain.

Staying together in one place and helping each other, men found that they had to remember many things — who owned what, who owed what, how this must be done, how that could be prevented. To help them remember, they drew pictures. Instead of laboriously carving on hard bone or stone, they could scratch their pictures into soft clay and bake it hard. The pictures grew simpler and easier. People agreed on what a few quickly scratched lines would stand for, and before 3000 B.C., somewhere in the heart of the Fertile Crescent, writing was invented.

History had begun.